AF479597

Meditations
for a
New Century

Essays
by
Lucy Ferriss

First Edition. Published by Wandering Aengus Press

Nonfiction
ISBN: 979-8-218-09090-6
Author Photo: Paul John Roberts
Book Design: Jill McCabe Johnson

Illustrations for "Meditation on Middle G" used by permission of artist Chloe Ferrone.

Wandering Aengus Press
PO Box 334 Eastsound, WA 98245
wanderingaenguspress.com

Wandering Aengus Press is dedicated to publishing works to enrich lives and make the world a better place.

Table of Contents

Introduction: Meditation on Meditations

The impulse for these essays was born in meditation. For decades I resisted the Western trend toward Buddhist sitting. The mind seemed to me designed for thought. The notion of emptying it of thought felt pointless. I would try plunking myself down, my legs in a clumsy half lotus, shutting my eyes and counting five breaths over and over for ten or twenty minutes. Nothing in my life changed, and I let the practice go. Only when blood-pressure concerns prompted me to explore routes toward calming my overactive heart did I give meditation another try. I have since found myself drawn, each day, toward spending a period of time dwelling within its given moment.

As a fiction writer, I have always been drawn toward the narrative arc, which pushes character and event toward their inevitable if unforeseen conclusion. In nonfiction, this impulse yields the persuasive or autobiographical essay—a span of prose meant either to change the reader's mind or create a story out of life materials. I wanted to resist this impulse. I wanted to do, in prose, what I did in sitting: to dwell on the thing, to find what happened when that stone dropped into the pond of my writing and the waves moved outward.

Famous books of meditations haven't always had this agenda. Descartes wished to argue for the rational basis of belief. Marcus Aurelius' *Meditations*, like the *Confessions* of Augustine and Rousseau, put autobiography in service to a philosophy of redemption. That is, these male authors related their past, often shameful exploits to guide them (and the reader) toward more ethical or God-fearing lives. More contemporary books, by the Dalai Lama or Thich Nhat Hanh, are meant to inspire.

The pieces that follow are more in the tradition of the *Essais* of Montaigne, with the emphasis on the French meaning of that title as "attempts" or "tests"—that is, nonlinear explorations beginning with the self but not necessarily ending there. Despite his expressed desire to make "myself the matter of this book," Montaigne occasionally drifted into didacticism, and it is altogether possible I've committed the same error. But just as he found a connection of method, if not of subject, between an essay like "On Smells" and one on "The Inequality Amongst Us," I have found myself inclined toward the small but receptive—with some trepidation—of the large.

Some of these were conceived and originally published as meditations. Others were published as essays, and it is only in looking back that I realized I was beginning to adopt the habit of dwelling that identifies them, to me, as meditative. Thus there is a range from more to less linear, from narrative to impressionistic; a range in the essays' ability to answer, or interest in answering, a question like "What is the point?" Some essays require more of the reader than others. In my experience, the more salient a narrative or persuasive arc, the more a reader can put herself in the writer's hands. When the point is not to make a point but to gather and concentrate one's attention until the thing blooms in the mind, the reader's active participation becomes an essential ingredient. We have to meet each other halfway.

For me, this project continues. Each effort engages anew in the tension between what the writer wants and what the subject calls for. These meditations are a start, an attempt, an *essai*.

Meditation on a Rat

The boy's version of *The king is dead! Long live the king!*: "Why'd you have to kill the dog? When do we get another one?"

For most of the seventeen years that Samba was alive, we thought of her as my husband's dog. A gift from a work colleague, she arrived one night when I was in bed with the flu, and by the time I recovered, she'd made herself at home. Only when I left my husband, moving to a new house, beginning a new job, and gaining full custody of our two prepubescent boys, did Samba become mine. Mine and the boys', that is. By this time, she had gone blind and incontinent. I didn't want her, but I couldn't let go of her either. One day, my husband found me cleaning up her mess in the front hall and insisted we put her down. She was his dog, he said, and he was making this decision.

We hadn't gotten divorced yet. I tunneled through the days. We hadn't killed the dog, I told the boys. We had kept her alive longer than nature would have, and now we had let her go. In her honor, we planted a dogwood in the backyard. "And you can get another dog," I went on, determined to limit my responsibilities, "when you have spent six months caring for a pet whose death I will not mourn."

Months went by. Just as I had with the dying marriage, I waited overlong. Each Sunday evening, my older son, Luke, the prime mover in the new-dog project, announced that he was ready for the pet store. Each Sunday I promised we'd go during the week, when the store was open. Then he forgot until the following Sunday. Finally he screwed up his courage on a Friday, and we drove to Fins & Feathers, where it was love at first sight—with a $250 ferret.

I amended the conditions. A pet whose death I would not mourn that cost less than $60. Thirty seconds of whining, then we moved on.

To the turtles, the fish, the canaries, the geckos and gerbils. There is no shopping quite so strange as small-pet shopping. Here's this plethora of carbon-based life forms yanked out of their environments, bred to withstand captivity, and assigned a price tag. Taking them home in their bowls and cages, we name them and foist on them the full weight of our anthropomorphism. We mistake their survival strategies for affection, their hunting or mating rituals for play and song, their bright or carefully camouflaged markings for adornment. They support a $60 billion industry, die young, and spread disease.

Luke considered a turtle with a neck like my grandfather's. He paused in front of a parrot that regarded him with ball-bearing eyes and refused to say he wanted a cracker. Finally he made his choice. For $20, a gray-and-white, pink-nosed baby rat.

"They're very smart creatures," the Fins & Feathers guy said, pulling the rat from its glass cage to show Luke. "He'll triple in size, but if you handle him regularly, he'll become very affectionate."

I wondered if they were trained to use the word *affectionate* about every creature in the shop. I watched the rat's tail, its hairless gray thickness, the wide, pale pink stripe midway down its length, the dry reptilian texture of the skin. "How long do they live?" I asked.

"Year and a half, if you're lucky," said the F&F guy.

"Maybe we can get two of them," Luke said, "and they can have babies."

"They're social creatures," said the guy.

"Mom?"

"I said *one* pet whose death I will not mourn."

The guy looked at me.

"It's an expression," I said.

"Well, it's hard to tell sometimes," said the guy, "if they're male or female."

"This one's a boy," Luke said, petting the thing behind its pinched ears. "I can tell."

I let Luke ask the questions about cage size, feeding, cleaning, handling. "So you're sure," I said, when we had assembled all the paraphernalia. "You want a pet rat."

"I'm naming him Skibber," Luke said.

"Why?"

"Because he looks like a Skibber, duh."

When Luke's brother, Dan, saw the rat, he said, "Ew," and then, "Cool." Luke cleared the top of his dresser, and Skibber moved in. Two weeks later, my husband and I put our marriage—shambling, blind, incontinent, beloved—out of its misery.

The breed of rat kept as a pet is known as a *fancy rat,* from the British idea of fancying an exotic pet. They were first bred in the nineteenth century for the blood sport of watching a terrier slaughter a corral full of them in record time. By the early twentieth century, pet rats were sitting on ladies' laps in the finest English households. Though their brains are smaller than those of their wild counterparts, they compensate with increased tolerance for noise, smells, crowding, and the other conditions of domesticated life.

Though I didn't have the horror response of our favorite babysitter, Alyssa, who would not set foot in Luke's room after Skibber moved in, I held the rat only a few times. I never felt comfortable with that tail draped over my wrist. Luke, however, wore Skibber around the house like a coonskin cap and brought Skibber to the dinner table. When I would not let the rat wander among the placemats, he perched on Luke's shoulder and ate the bits of lettuce and broccoli that Luke passed his way. Both boys liked to do their homework in the living room, and often Luke deposited Skibber in the potted plant by the sofa, where he nested in the dirt. I would go to turn out the light and have to call up the stairs, "Luke! Come get your rat!" Though I told myself I would not mourn the death of Skibber, I was not eager to discover him dead under the piano at the end of a trail of rat shit.

As a draw for neighborhood boys, Skibber was unparalleled. Both Luke and Dan got street cred by pulling Skibber out of his cage and passing him around. "Your mom lets you keep a rat?" the other boys asked, impressed.

"Sure," my guys said. "We're getting a dog soon," they said. Or, "We used to have a dog," but the other boys didn't seem interested in news of a dog.

"Can it do tricks?" they asked.

"Making rats do tricks is mean," Luke said with authority.

"My mom'd freak out," one boy said.

"What if you got a mouse to keep it company? Would it kill a mouse? That'd be cool, to watch it kill a mouse."

"Skibber," Luke said, holding the rat on his flat palm, stroking it with one finger from head to tail, "wouldn't kill anything. He's a vegetarian."

"He's my rat, too," Dan sometimes said, and to my surprise Luke let him take Skibber to pass around his own circle of friends, down in the basement. Dan liked to set up mazes for Skibber, usually with a chunk of cheese at the end. I'd wander downstairs to see a dozen boys peering over the walls of books and planks. When Skibber hit a dead end, he would sniff the air and begin licking his paws. Eventually Dan would turn him around and nudge him through the labyrinth again. "He's not hungry enough," Dan would complain when his friends grew bored with the performance.

"We're not going to starve him," Luke said.

Sometimes Luke took the cage out to the middle of a broad field across the road from us. I'd stand at the front window and watch him open the cage, coax the rat, then finally reach in and pull Skibber out. He'd set him down in the long grass and kneel alongside or stretch out on his belly. After ten minutes, they'd return. "Skibber doesn't understand he's free," Luke said. "I want him to run in the field. He should get exercise."

"Luke, a rat in the middle of a field is a target for a hawk. Skibber knows that. He's frightened in the field, he wants to hide."

"I wouldn't let a hawk get him."

"He doesn't know that."

"He should trust me."

How peculiar it is, this business of pet owning. One mother I know gave in to her son's begging for a boa constrictor. Snakes need to be handled regularly lest they become aggressive, so when the kid lost interest, she began wearing the snake around the house as she picked up toys or cooked dinner. Once, she forgot and answered the door draped in snake. Other families we knew cultivated iguanas, gerbils, a monkey, a pony, a mongoose. In the boys' younger years, in addition to the dog, we'd made our way through a chameleon, two betta fish, a passel of goldfish, and a brief series of rabbits. Caring for a pet is supposed to be a healthy experience for a child. Animal care is frequently prescribed to help people with mental illness learn empathy and acceptance. But we know nothing of how the animals feel about this relationship. In the philosopher Thomas Nagel's famous essay "What Is It Like to Be a Bat?" he proposes that "Our own experience provides the basic material for our imagination, whose range is therefore limited. It will not help to try to imagine that one has webbing on one's arms … and that one spends the day hanging upside down." But at least we know that the animal Nagel is discussing exists in its natural environment, where the usual needs for food, shelter, and reproduction apply.

For the animals we keep, none of these imperatives holds. Moreover, most of these animals have been bred, like Skibber, to be more accommodating to our needs. Bearing only a distant family relationship to animals found in forest or stream, they exist more as a fulfillment of human wish than as animals in themselves. Although Nagel asks rhetorically, "What would be left of what it was like to be a bat if one removed the viewpoint of the bat?" he doesn't address the notion that we are engineering creatures whose subjectivity is inextricably bound with their altered biology.

So maybe a word like *trust* can be applied to a creature like Skibber, or maybe not. Maybe he feels his cage is a home; maybe he feels imprisoned, whatever that means for a rat. In the Rat Park experiments of the 1970s, rats living in an "enriched environment"— with male-female colonies, plenty of space, and ample amusement— proved immune to morphine addiction, whereas caged rats took to the drug with gusto. That this stark difference conveyed a message for humans about social conditions and heroin addiction seems irrefutable. But analogizing Rat Park as Utopia and the cage as the slum doesn't mean that Skibber experiences anything like, say, the rat Bigger Thomas aims to kill in Richard Wright's *Native Son*. When Wright tells us that the rat "emitted a long thin song of defiance," he is foreshadowing Bigger's own entrapment and dehumanization, yet does the rat defy anything? Can it sing?

Six months went by, eight, ten. Luke turned fourteen. He cleaned Skibber's cage, kept his water bottle filled, dispensed food and treats, reminded me when he was low on supplies. If he slept over at a friend's house, the cage moved to Dan's room. The system was perfect. Maybe, I thought, a rat was enough. Maybe they had forgotten about the dog. This was fine with me. I had never been a so-called dog person. I'd spent much of my childhood overcoming a keen fear of dogs.

Then one Sunday night, Luke looked at the calendar and counted the months. "Hey, Mom," he said, "let's go to the pound."

                    Meditations for a New Century

"They're closed right now, honey," I said. "We'll go during the week."

The pattern reestablished itself—Sunday night bids followed by a week's worth of reluctance—until, after Skibber had been with us well over a year, Luke thought of the pound on a Thursday afternoon. With a queasy sense of dread, I kept my part of the bargain. We came home with a terrier puppy that the boys named Bernie, after one of their favorite NBA players.

Luke was now taller than I was. He'd started to be interested in girls. Dan was blossoming into a fiercely competitive athlete, with a travel schedule and practice every afternoon. I had been a single parent for two years and saw a steep climb still ahead. "You can make up a schedule for Bernie," I suggested, as we set him up with chew toys and pee paper. "One of you walks him in the morning, the other at night. Or whatever you boys decide. Just scoop the poop and be sure he's got fresh water at home."

It was late October when we took Bernie on his first tour of the neighborhood. The nights had gone cool and dry; leaves carpeted the lawn. Luke unhooked the dog from his leash, leaned down and hugged him. When he'd straightened, he hugged me. "Now we have a dog," he said. "Now we're a family again."

And I knew that, whatever responsibility I might try to assign for the dog, my fate was sealed. I could refuse to mourn a rat. A family was different.

As for Skibber, the boys were determined that he and Bernie would be pals. Terriers, I pointed out, are bred to hunt rats. One snap of Bernie's jaws would spell the end of Skibber. The prospect of rescuing Skibber at the last moment tantalized them, but I foresaw disaster. I called the vet. How old is the dog? he wanted to know. Had Bernie seen the rat in its cage? Had he smelled the rat? Well then, he said to my surprise, they should be fine.

And they were. The boys set them up on Dan's bed, with blankets and pillows pushed to the side. Bernie shoved his nose aggressively underneath the reptilian tail, and Skibber regarded him with the patience of an elder whose clumsy grandson is being a nuisance. Luke and Dan squealed like the children they were rapidly leaving behind. When Bernie began batting at Skibber with his paw, they put him back in the cage and went off to call their friends.

What I thought was the end came one day about three months after Bernie moved in. Luke called me at work. Something was wrong with Skibber. He was walking funny. His head was shaking. No, Luke hadn't taken him out of his cage. No one had handled him.

"He's had a stroke," I said when I came home to find the rat gimping around the side of his cage, his head cocked oddly and bobbing repeatedly.

"How do you know?" asked Dan. "You're not a doctor."

"I've seen strokes," I said with adult-simulated confidence.

"Is he hurting?" Luke asked.

One of the debates that roll on about nonhuman animals is the degree to which they suffer. Feeling pain, apparently, is one thing, suffering another. It presumably involves some awareness of pain, perhaps some sense of time—that is, I suffer from this headache because it has gone on and on, whereas an ant with an injured leg may avoid walking on that leg because it increases the pain, but the ant has no awareness of the pain's persistence and so does not suffer. If we could just breed the suffering out of chickens and cows, some argue, we could bring many vegetarians back into the carnivorous fold. Luke was asking, I think, whether Skibber was suffering.

I hedged. I thought of Samba, the cataracts clouding her eyes. Friends had advised me, as my marriage slowly frayed, that a clean break would be better all around. Fewer lingering doubts, less scar tissue, less suffering. "Skibber's lived a lot longer than he was supposed to," I said. "I think this is his way of telling us he's ready to go."

"Go where?" said Dan.

"She means die, stupid," said Luke. Then he fixed me with his stare, a vampirish scowl he'd picked up from the movies. "You're not killing him, too," he said.

"What I think would be kindest," I said, "would be to let him go into the woods. That's where he wants to be. I mean, he's a rat. He'll just go somewhere quiet and die peacefully, on his own terms."

"Maybe the vet can fix him," said Dan, watching Skibber round the corner of his cage, Quasimodo on four legs.

"I don't know if the vet treats rats," I said.

"You could ask."

"I could."

"When you asked about Bernie and Skibber being friends, the

                    Meditations for a New Century

vet said you were wrong."

I took a deep breath. The boys were fifteen and thirteen now. Already the lesson of this whole experiment was fading: I took Bernie for his nightly walks, I kept his water bowl filled. "But you remember our deal," I said. "Skibber is your pet. If you want him to go to the vet, you need to arrange that."

"You mean pay for it," said Luke.

I nodded. Luke locked eyes with Dan, who was better at hoarding the cash from allowances and odd jobs. "How much?" said Dan.

I gave them the number of the vet, and Luke called—$65, he reported, for an office visit and exam. Dan put up $40, Luke $25. The first appointment they could get was the next morning, when they were in school. "All right," I relented. "I'll take him. But if the vet says I'm right, that there's nothing to do for Skibber, do you want me to leave him there?"

Luke had gone with his dad to be with Samba when she was "put down." I had not been at all sure this was a good idea, but forbidding it raised a specter of the unknown that was almost equally disturbing. He'd come home rattled. She was there, Luke had said to me that night, holding my hand before he fell asleep, and then she wasn't there anymore. I thought it would be different, he'd said, and tears ran down his cheeks.

Now he conferred with Dan. No, they said. If the vet says Skibber must die, bring him home and we'll let him go in the woods, like you said.

Thus I found myself sitting in the veterinary waiting room with $65 worth of crumpled small bills in my pocket and a cage with a stroke-ridden rat on the bench next to me. When I was called in to the examining room, I apologized. The vet confirmed that the rat had had a stroke. "But is he eating?" he asked.

"He ate some yesterday."

"Drinking?"

I nodded. He set the cage on the floor and pulled out the rat. Skibber bobbed and gimped his way around the examining room. "He's fine," the vet said.

"But he's had a stroke!"

"Sure. People have strokes, too. And they go on living."

The real end came a few weeks later, while I was out of town with Dan at a tennis tournament. Alyssa was babysitting. On the phone Luke reported that he'd come home from his summer program to find Skibber motionless. "Aw, honey," I said. "I'm so sorry."

"It's okay. He died peacefully. But I don't know what to do."

"Do you feel up to burying him?"

"Not by myself."

Alyssa, I knew, would not touch the rat. I told Luke to put the cage in the basement, where it was cooler; I'd take care of it in three days, when we got home. Dan, texting his friends, looked up to say he would miss Skibber. By the time we returned, both he and Luke seemed to have forgotten about the death. I descended to the basement and flicked on the fluorescent light. Skibber's cage was in the corner, behind what was left of one of the old mazes Dan used to construct. Deflated, Skibber lay on the floor like a rat-skin rug. As I drew closer, I saw the maggots going in and out of his eye sockets. I clamped my lips over my scream. Quickly I carried the cage upstairs, through the kitchen, and around the corner of the backyard.

Dan was upstairs unpacking; Luke was playing a video game. "Was that Skibber?" he asked when I came back inside to hunt for a trowel.

"Yes, honey. I don't think you want to see him."

He paused the game and looked at me. "I guess not," he said when he saw whatever he saw in my face.

"I'm going to bury him," I said.

"Thanks, Mom."

We didn't discuss whether disposing of the carcass was part of being responsible for a pet whose death your mother would not mourn. Dan, I gathered, thought Skibber had already been buried. But I felt unexpectedly terrible as I reached inside the cage with the trowel to pull out Skibber's infested body and lay it in the hole under the dogwood. It seemed wrong to have let him rot like that, for four days unburied. Despite my best efforts, the rat had awakened in me that familiar, unsettling sense of sympathy.

I don't recall what happened to Skibber's cage, his bottle, or his bag of kibble. He would be the last penned-up animal with whom I would cohabit. The dog has lingered—living long, as mutts do, while my boys have grown up and moved away. Now my partner and I take turns walking him at night; we bemoan the cost of kenneling him when we're out of town. For a while, my partner pointed out that since neither he nor I wanted a dog, Bernie might be happier in a home with kids who would play with him. Maybe he would, maybe he wouldn't—what is it like to be a dog? Either way, I can't relinquish that which made my boys and me a family again. Luke and Dan expect, when they come home, that both Mom and the dog will greet them with sustained and unbounded ecstasy.

The morning after I buried Skibber, I was standing at the kitchen window with a cup of coffee and noticed Bernie frolicking about the backyard. This was no ball or stick he was playing with. Luke and Dan were still asleep, and I ran out barefoot, in my bathrobe, and shooed the dog away from the quarry he had dug up. Then I took hold of the rat by its handy tail and flung it over the fence, into a neighboring copse. I slapped my hands clean and went inside, leaving the dog panting, his memory of his playmate erased like a cartoon on a chalkboard, the transitory stuff of our imaginings.

Meditation on Pain

About every six seconds someone stabs me in the middle of my back, just left of my spine. He stabs with a short, thick dagger, which he twists once, maybe twice before pulling it out. Six seconds later, same thing. With each stab, my breath stops short. Breathe, I tell myself, breathe. I try not to cry out. Crying out sinks the dagger deeper.

Sometimes it's not a dagger. Sometimes it's a mouth. A mouth of pain. About the size of a toddler's mouth, it presses its lips together, holding the pain in, for six seconds. Then the little toddler lips open, and inside blooms red, screaming, gums and lips and tongue and little white teeth of pure pain. The lips close again, count to six, open.

The first time this happened to me, I thought I had pulled a muscle. I managed to drive to the walk-in clinic, where the doctor asked me to touch my toes. When I did, he told me I couldn't be that flexible with a pulled muscle. I had shingles, he said. He prescribed antiviral drugs, for which I was deeply grateful. The only other time I had had shingles was in the 1980s, before the antivirals were available. I'd had a new boyfriend, who was horrified by the rash spreading down my torso, my arm, my hip. Everything ached, I remember, but I couldn't let my skin be touched. The shingles lasted seven weeks, three weeks longer than the boyfriend.

Now the dagger sank only into this particular spot on my back, no rash emerged, and nothing spread. But by the time I'd filled the prescription, the dagger was twisting; the mouth of pain was opening, shutting, opening. I couldn't walk properly. Half-bent, crying out with each step, I made it to the bathroom and wept on the toilet. I took the antivirals. I dug out a vial of hydrocodone, from my older son's wisdom tooth extraction. My husband rolled the TV set into the living room, where I lay on my side on the couch, zonked on opiates, glugging brandy, and watching *Beasts of the Southern Wild*. I understood nothing of the story—only the rain, the wind and fire, that beneficent feral little girl, the melting ice caps, the roaring animals.

Like the waters, the pain receded after three days. A month later, it came again. Ten months later, again, and again three weeks after I finished the antivirals. Shingles, the doctors said. Meanwhile, I'd started getting headaches, on the left side of my head at the back, every two months or so, that lasted almost two weeks without ceasing. The doctors called these migraines, or tension, or occipital neuralgia. The pain would not let me sleep, I told them. They regarded me skeptically. I get cavities filled, I told them, without Novocain. When I broke my wrist, I didn't even realize it. My pain threshold is quite high.

On a scale of one to ten, they ask me. We have conceived this scale, perhaps, in response to the conundrum framed by Virginia Woolf:

> Let a sufferer try to describe a pain in his head to a doctor and language at once runs dry. There is nothing ready made for him. He is forced to coin words himself, and, taking his pain in one hand, and a lump of pure sound in the other (as perhaps the people of Babel did in the beginning), so to crush them together that a brand-new word in the end drops out.

A doctor's office is not the place for brand-new words. It is the place for numbers. The scale gives suggestions: ten is "the worst pain you can imagine." If I choose ten, am I dying? But dying, experts say, can be painless. A heart attack, a simple cramp in the chest, then the release of breath and it's over. So think childbirth, but I can't. Not because I've forgotten, the way received wisdom says we do, but because birthing pain was labor, was work, was aimed at producing something. The mouth of pain in my back opens and closes and says nothing, and I cannot feed it, it will not be satisfied. "I have discovered," Eula Biss writes, "that the pain I am in is always the worst pain imaginable." But I do not want to insult the monster afflicting me by supposing that he cannot up the ante. I circle "9."

Over the years the doctors have prescribed anti-seizure medications, gabapentin and amitriptyline. They have prescribed muscle relaxants, anti-inflammatories, migraine drugs, more opiates. They have ordered scans. They've sent me to physical therapy. I've tried chiropractic, acupuncture, massage, biofeedback.

One minute you're a member of the body politic. The next, you're a body, a receptacle for pharmaceuticals and an endless bore at the few parties you still attend. Each time you try a new doctor, he squints, certain you must be telling him the same thing he's heard before, only using different words. The nurse practitioners keep asking: Are you sure you're not sensitive to light? to noise? Are you sure you don't get nauseated? Okay, you finally admit, the pain is horrendous. With that kind of pain, you don't want bright lights or loud noises, and you sure as hell can't eat anything. Now they've got you. The doctor comes in, looks at the chart, says, Uh-huh, photosensitivity, aural sensitivity, it's a migraine. Migraines, you remind him, last a couple of days at the outside. This headache lasts two weeks. Right, he says. Couple days more or less. You've got a migraine.

But the stabbing in the back, you say. That came on suddenly and lasted three days before the antivirals kicked it in the balls, and as soon as it left the headache came on.

They send you to an infectious disease specialist, who says it's herpes simplex, not the herpes zoster that causes shingles. She asks you questions about the time you had genital herpes. Only you've never had genital herpes, you keep telling her. You can hardly say the word, *herpes.* It's such an ugly word. Puts you in mind of herpetologists, those people who study slimy, crawly things, and in fact it comes from the same Greek word meaning *to creep.* When you deny your herpes, the doctor regards you skeptically. You can't even remember having had a cold sore, but sure enough, the titer for herpes simplex shows up in your blood, and that nails it as far as she's concerned. *To creep.* She puts you on a prophylactic dose of antivirals. A week later, you get a headache. Three months later, the back-stabbing thing, then the headache.

I'm switching back to first person because this happens to me, not to you. Everyone who tells me, *Oh, I get that too!* narrates a story of muscle spasm, slipped disc, migraine. These things are awful. They are not the same. I am jealous of my pain. I will not have it made common, not after all these doctors, all these failed cures. I will not share it.

When the stabbing gets worse, maybe sixteen hours into the attack, I try to lie very, very still. I lie on my right side, my knees clutching a pillow and my hands tucked under my chin. At first I try to read this way—I've got classes to prep for—but moving my hand to turn the page of the book brings on a sharp stab and a deep twist of the knife. If I raise my head, a scream rips from my throat. I give up and shut my eyes. I focus on my breathing, to keep it shallow. When my husband comes in to ask if he can do anything, I wait until I've inhaled. Then I say, "No, thanks, honey, I'm lying still," all in one exhale. The pain usually grabs me midway through that sentence anyhow, but I try to fool it. If I have to blow my nose or scratch the itch in my temple, I wait until a spasm of pain has hit and then I act, since the spasm's there already.

After I lie still as a stone for twenty minutes, the pain subsides. Now it's just the toddler mouth, opening to its red horror in the middle of my back, then closing again, all while I keep the breathing steady, shallow. I wait as long as possible before getting up to pee, because then all hell breaks loose—*Ha! Ha! Gotcha! Stab! Stab! Stab and twist! Awwoo*—while I stumble to the bathroom, let down a yellow stream, stumble back, and lie in bed weeping and cursing the Old Testament God in whom I now fervently believe.

My husband warms up the vibrating massage tool he bought on Amazon and runs it up and down my back, up and down, up and down. The thrumming goes deep into the nerve. For maybe ten blissful minutes, I sleep.

Our poets of pain are Donne, who lay gripped by malaria; Kafka, who died of starvation; Dickinson with her strabismus; Fanny Burney, who endured a mastectomy awake and without anesthetic. Here's Donne, wishing he were paying the debt for pleasure:

> 'Cause I did suffer I must suffer pain.
> Th' hydropic drunkard, and night-scouting thief,
> The itchy lecher, and self-tickling proud
> Have the remembrance of past joys for relief
> Of comming ills. To (poor) me is allowed
> No ease

Oh, you self-pitier, you Christian fool. Thinking that pain ought to be payment, ought to be just. Give me Dickinson, who suffered from God knows what, but took suffering on its own terms:

> Pain has an element of blank;
> It cannot recollect
> When it began, or if there were
> A day when it was not.
>
> It has no future but itself,

> Its infinite realms contain
> Its past, enlightened to perceive
> New periods of pain.

As I lie stone-still, inhabiting my wracked body like a prisoner on a ship in a cyclone, I enter Dickinson's world: no memory of anything before the pain, no future without it. I am afraid of death. Yet if someone in authority were to say to me, in the midst of the four worst days, "This is the shape of the rest of your life," I would put a bullet into my brain without thinking twice about it.

Perhaps it's this stark choice, pain or death, that draws writers to pain like moths to flame. Kafka must have found pain erotic or he could not have written "In the Penal Colony," with its "apparatus" inscribing the sentence upon the body of the condemned, who "for the first six hours . . . goes on living almost as before. He suffers nothing but pain. After two hours, the felt is removed, for at that point the man has no more energy for screaming." Pain seduces language even more than sex does, for language must and will articulate—and yet where, amid this crystallized sensation, oh where do we find the words? Fanny Burney comes as close as any, in her description of her mastectomy:

> when the dreadful steel was plunged into the breast—cutting through veins—arteries—flesh—nerves—I needed no injunctions not to restrain my cries. I began a scream that lasted unintermittingly during the whole time of the incision—and I almost marvel that it rings not in my Ears still! so excruciating was the agony. When the wound was made, and the instrument was withdrawn, the pain seemed undiminished, for the air that suddenly rushed into those delicate parts felt like a mass of minute but sharp and forked poniards, that were tearing the edges of the wound—but when again I felt the instrument—describing a curve—cutting against the grain, if I may so say, while the flesh resisted in a manner so forcible as to oppose and tire the hand of the operator, who was forced to change from the right to the left— then, indeed, I thought I must have expired.

And yet it's not enough. For pain is like consciousness: we have only our own and cannot genuinely imagine another. I try and fail to climb inside Burney's pain; in fact, I lock onto the words as a way of abstracting the very thing she is trying to describe. The critic Elaine

Scarry claims that the body in pain is unrepresentable, but I suspect that's because language suffers a gap between writer and reader. Every pain is newborn and gropes for its outlines. Stabbed in the back, I lunge forward. My chest jerks up. My face contorts. A glottal *ungh* squeezes from my throat. If you're near me, your own mouth goes dry. If you care even a smidge about me, something hurtles through your own body. Rousseau tagged that "natural pity" as "a virtue [that] precedes the exercise of all reflection," a discourse we share with the beasts he extolled.

The body, then, represents its pain quite nicely; it's only words that fall short. Woolf again: "English, which can express the thoughts of Hamlet and the tragedy of Lear, has no words for the shiver and the headache." Words are the cages in which we contain our monsters, and we cannot capture pain. We long to lock it down, hold it in place, study it. As if we could say, *This is what I went through*, and then it could never defeat us. Otherwise, we fear that the next time, the pain will destroy us. "Pain," said Albert Schweitzer, "is a more terrible lord of mankind than death itself." Statistics don't capture pain. What good is it to say that more Americans suffer from chronic pain than from heart disease, diabetes, and cancer combined, when plenty of that pain comes with cancer? What good to detail the amount of money we spend on pain management, especially if we also learn that more than half of pain sufferers feel they have no control over their pain? Buck up, people! Lose the weight that gives you the low back pain! Stretch that neck! Statistics explain our opioid epidemic, sure. I have a nice little stash of Tramadol, hydrocodone, oxycodone, and Tylenol with codeine in the bottom drawer. When they're gone, well, I don't know. If I could capture the religious intensity of this pain, I imagine, I might meditate on it, determine how to navigate it on my own next time.

Then the pain passes. After a week, after a fortnight, I grow buoyant. I walk in the nectar of sunshine. I feel cleansed, innocent. "It has been said," wrote Thomas Hardy, "that mere ease after torment is delight for a time." Woolf finds the release from pain close to reincarnation:

> We go down in the pit of death and feel the waters of annihilation close above our heads and wake thinking to find ourselves in the presence of the angels and the harpers when we have a tooth out and come to the surface in the dentist's arm-chair and confuse his "Rinse the mouth—rinse the

mouth" with the greeting of the Deity stooping from the floor of Heaven to welcome us.

Is this the function of pain? To yield delight in the unstuttered breath, the breach of the abscess, the sealing of the mouth of pain, the dagger-free skull, the body erect?

No. The possibility remains that one day, the pain will not cease. I know from statistics that I share this fear: A majority of Americans report a rise in anxiety associated with pain. The function of pain is to signal trouble. If the trouble is phantom, or incurable, nothing redeems the stubborn fact of physical torment. Dickinson, again, comes closer to the real bond between pain and its aftermath. "After great pain," she begins one poem, "a formal feeling comes." Calm, free for the moment, she pays respect to the gauntlet she's run without invoking any romance:

> This is the Hour of Lead—
> Remembered, if outlived,
> As Freezing persons, recollect the Snow—
> First—Chill—then Stupor—then the letting go—

"*If* outlived." Each time, the thought crosses my constricted mind: I will not survive this. It is not the pain we remember, Dickinson tells us, but the form the pain takes. "The Nerves sit Ceremonious," she writes, "like Tombs." We arrange ourselves, knowing in our secret hearts that all form collapsed within the pain, that we succumbed, that we were—for a time—not beings but qualities.

When I was a girl, I had a series of masochistic dreams. Each of them began with my approaching a little man, a sort of Rumpelstiltskin, on a street corner, and asking him to give me the dream. Then I would be plunged into a trial. I ran barefoot over burning grass, my lungs exploding. A mob lifted me and tossed me over a cliff into a rushing cataract. I clawed my way up a cliff while a volley of arrows pierced my back. I stood bound to a stake as the oily torch lit the tinder at my feet. When the dream became too frightening, I had to do the hardest thing: I had to shut my eyes in the face of the terror. When I opened them again, I would be in another dream, not a masochistic dream but an ordinary child's dream of floating or flying. I told no one of these dreams; I knew they meant something was wrong with me.

When I first began suffering from this pain—we'll call it herpes, however much I hate the word—as an adult, I wondered if I

                    Meditations for a New Century

were somehow bringing it on myself, the way I used to bring on those dreams. But as I lie there, unmoving, guarding my breath, I remember that in none of the childhood dreams did I experience pain. I was proving to myself, for whatever quirky reason, that I was tough. I could stand the fire, the ice. I could stare danger in the face and then shut my eyes to it. But physically, I felt, or dreamed, nothing actually painful. Whatever afflicts me now brings unquestionably the most intense sensation my body has ever known and may ever know. Sensation so exquisite that its memory dissipates the moment my attacker releases the vibrating nerve. But I want neither the pain nor the delight of its ease. I am tough enough. The poetry of pain desecrates the world.

Meditation on Needlepoint

Insofar as religion concerns a theory of an afterlife—and let's face it, anything else amounts to philosophy—I lost what remained of my religious faith when I inherited my mother's needlepoint purse.

The purse is what we used to call a clutch. I remember it as my mother's go-to bag from my earliest childhood to adolescence. I know she crafted it herself because she included her initials, AHF, in the corner, in green yarn embedded in the backdrop of black. The main design is a stylized tree, in almond brown, with green and yellow leaves curling out from the candelabra branches. A few touches of gold, in the shape of pears, punctuate the black. For a clutch, the purse is capacious, bladdering out from the gold rim that snaps together at the top. My mother lined it in green and stitched in a little pocket for her comb, which still nestles within.

My mother was a whiz with a needle. Early one fourth-grade morning, I burst into my parents' bedroom with the panicked news that I had forgotten an assignment for which we'd had a week to prepare. I needed to be at school in two hours costumed as a Greek goddess. Which goddess? my mother wanted to know, rubbing her eyes and reaching for her cigarettes.

Demeter, I said. Goddess of nature.

Within an hour, my mother had taken down a curtain in the sewing room (formerly my brother's bedroom; he'd decamped to the attic) and stitched it into a toga with a Greek-key design at the hem. She'd rummaged through a chest and found various fronds of plastic leaves and flowers and stitched them onto a plastic headband swathed in a torn nylon stocking. She'd dressed up my sneakers with green and gold rickrack. Later that day, I took first prize in the Greek mythology dress-up contest.

My mother also knitted, needles silently worrying the yarn that looped its way into our sweaters and scarves. She'd learned to knit as a tubercular child, in Chicago, where the cure at the children's hospital involved strategies like having her sleep out on the roof in midwinter, snow falling on the mound of blankets over her slight body, in the hope of freezing out the tubercles. She wasn't allowed to read; mental activity was thought to rouse the disease. But she could work her hands, and her mother brought in brightly colored yarns for her to knit into scarves for the other afflicted children.

But needlepoint was the tapestry of my mother's time. I went with her to the shop in town that sold patterns and yarns, and watched as she contemplated her next project. A seat cushion, even for a needleworker like my mother, could take months. The pews on which we knelt, at our huge gothic Episcopal church, had been needlepointed by the Women's Guild. My mother, being an atheist, was not a member, but everyone knew that the project had consumed the energy and skills of perhaps two dozen women for the better part of five years.

Needlepoint patterns were not cheap, so sometimes my mother drew her own on the stiff white canvas. I don't know if the tree of her clutch was a design she bought or created. I vaguely remember her working on it. I remember wishing it were brighter—lime or melon—not this deep black background with the tan tree. But my mother was a sophisticate. She admired Chagall and Van Gogh. When she worked her tiny Wilcox & Gibbs chain-stitch sewing machine, it was to create knockoffs of dresses she'd seen in *Vogue*. She spent up to $15, in the 1960s, for the fabrics and patterns that would yield an outfit others would see as designer label. She taught me to sew as well, of course, and I tried making blouses with overlapping tucks either side of the front placket, like the rich girls were buying at Honeybee boutique. My tucks always came out a little crooked, but for once I didn't mind the teasing, because I knew what my mother was capable of. I had a goal.

Sewing clothes saved money. Today, sweat shops in Asia flood our markets with inexpensive and often well-made goods. But in my childhood and my mother's active adulthood, being handy with a needle was a useful skill for a middle-class woman. Ditto knitting, in an era when "virgin wool" was coveted and pricey while polyester meant thin, cheap, and bound to pill. We were long past the early nineteenth century in which Mary Lamb lamented that "tedious work" of which she wrote, "I know not a single family where there is not some essential drawback to its comfort which may be traced to needlework done at home . . . for which no remuneration in money is received." But it would still have been possible to calculate, as Lamb suggests, "how much money has been saved by needle-work done in the family."

Needlepoint was another matter. No one needed needlepoint. Yes, the tight stitching of wool in and around an interlock canvas made for a durable surface. Yes, the dyed-in colors held faster than printed ones. But in no universe did such advantages outweigh the enormous investment these items required. As Lamb noted two centuries ago, needlepoint was "so long in the operation that purchasing the labour has seldom been thought good economy." Instead, needlepoint took a step toward the boundaries separating skill from craft and craft from art. The patterns (unless you drew your own) were given—but you chose the one that reflected your aesthetic vision, and you were free to add elements, like the initials my mother wove into the corner of her clutch. Perhaps most important, creating a pillowcase, a purse, a belt, or a set of seat cushions out of needlepoint suggested that your ample leisure time was devoted to creative work.

I learned to do needlepoint the way I learned ballroom dancing and the proper arrangement of silver flatware for a four-course dinner—that is, as a talent whose usefulness would predecease my proficiency. The reasons are obvious. I grew up amid the second wave of feminism. I assumed I would at least work, at best pursue a profession. In the seesaw between valuing traditional female pursuits and trying to beat men at their game, I inclined toward the latter. But even if I hadn't, the very need to justify and value so-called women's work meant highlighting its essential nature: a child's need for its mother, the superiority of home-cooked food and family dinnertimes, the role of women in philanthropy. Needlepoint had no more place in the argument than it did for the pioneering astronomer Maria Mitchell, who wrote that "the eye that directs a needle in the delicate meshes of embroidery will equally well bisect a star with the spider web of the micrometer."

Needlepoint hasn't entirely disappeared. At craft chain stores like Michaels and JOANN, you can find needlepoint kits at upwards of $150 for pillow covers reading "Home Sweet Home" and the like. I assume some women buy and work these kits. But the sight of a needlepointed clutch purse on Fifth Avenue would convince most of us that we had entered a time warp.

                    Meditations for a New Century

Which brings me to religion. Also, by way of tangent, to needle phobia. But let's take religion first, since I began with that bait.

Every morning now, I wake to the sight of my mother's needlepoint clutch, which sits in a useless little alcove in our bedroom wall. I note its lack of handles: it cannot be carried into the world without putting one hand out of commission or clapping one upper arm against the ribs to secure the thing. I see my mother shoving it under her arm, a scarf over the curlers on her head, charging out the back door on her way to pick up my younger sister at nursery school. I see her at age nine in the children's sanitarium in Chicago, receiving the news that her father, hospitalized for months in the adult sanitarium across town, has died, and that she will not be allowed out of the hospital for the funeral. I see her going to work for IBM during the war. I see her turning down a marriage proposal from the love of her life because her contract at IBM specified that she had to resign if she became engaged, and she knew she couldn't bear the hardscrabble life that would be hers on her beloved's truck-driver salary. I hear her telling us children that when the Russians dropped atomic bombs on the Midwest, we could not bring our cat to the bomb shelter in the back yard. I see how deeply her terror of Communism infused her loyalty to a Republican party that claimed we were battling that scourge on the far side of the world, in Vietnam. I hear her asking my dad for permission to return to work. I feel her shame at her eventual divorce, the way it cut her off from what she would have called polite society. I contemplate the careful crafting of that needlepoint clutch, and I recall my mother's lifelong disgust with sex, a disgust more normal than deviant, given the ways in which the men and women among whom she grew up coped with each other and with female sexuality.

In short, I cannot separate the mother I loved from the historical frame of her life, the same frame that dictated her owning a clutch purse, a purse she might needlepoint herself. She died in 2004. What good is it to ask, for instance, what she would have thought of Donald Trump? My mother was politically aware, even passionate. But any view would have had to be shaped by living through the second half of Bush II, through the Obama administration, through the rise of social media—and she missed out on all that. To endow her with some sort of spiritual life that would continue past 2004 is to posit some identity for her that isn't governed by historical circumstance. And as much as I loved her for the talented, acerbic, clever, vulnerable person she was, without that circumstance she has no identity at all.

Neither do any of us.

In his brilliant, empathic novel *Lincoln in the Bardo*, George Saunders creates a world of limbo, in which ectoplasmic characters in the graveyard where Willie Lincoln is buried try to help him get across to some other metaphysical place. I don't know if Saunders wrestled with this question of identity, history, the afterlife. Fortunately for the conceit of the novel, the cemetery is American, nineteenth century; its inhabitants, though they don't seem to know who Lincoln is, are all fairly recently deceased. They are not so much in an afterlife as in an unresolved, death-afflicted life. Hence the bardo, which derives from a Buddhist concept of the intermediate stage between two lives *on earth*—that is, lives that will each be lived within some short span of history. All the characters in Saunders' bardo have died within the previous couple of decades. When the spirit of Jane Ellis, for instance, recounts how "Once at the Christmastide Papa took us to a wonderful village festival," we twenty-first-century readers detect a nineteenth-century voice. What lies beyond the bardo of the novel, after a much-desired "matterlightblooming phenomenon," Saunders does not speculate. It could be, like any existence untethered to history, a complete nullity.

That's what I think when I look at my mother's needlepointed clutch: that she has to be truly dead, nonexistent, because she could exist only as a woman who would needlepoint that particular abstract, stylized, Modernist purse in the early 1960s, that hinge in the twentieth century. A woman born in 1922, dead in 2004.

Needle-phobia tangent: I cope with a primal terror of needles entering my bloodstream. I'm not afraid of blood, nor do I have an issue with, say, acupuncture needles, which neither draw blood from my body nor inject some substance into my veins. When movies depict heroin addicts shooting up or patients getting IVs, I have to shut my eyes. I've been able to have blood drawn only by giving the phlebotomist specific directions about what to say and not say to me while I keep my head averted and bite my thumb.

I believe this phobia derives from the story of Robin Hood. I was obsessed, as a child, with stories of medieval England, from

                    Meditations for a New Century

Arthur and the Round Table up through the Wars of the Roses. In the attic of our house, before my brother moved up there, we found a box of lead figures of knights that I immediately claimed. My mother gave me the tiny wooden baskets in which the A&P sold strawberries and cherry tomatoes, to stack into castles and keeps. I would like to claim this passion individually, as it were—to credit it to my own romanticism and my budding interest in the structure of myth and story. But the fact is that, as a child of the genteel middle class, I lived in a house full of books handed down from the generation that, in the late nineteenth century, first flaunted their wealth by way of crowded bookshelves in living rooms. Classics of Victorian children's literature and the works of Sir Walter Scott, so treasured by the fallen aristocracy of the post-bellum South, marched across our walls. I have a few of those books now, and my bookshelves sag under the weight of my own purchases over the years. But my children grew up in a world of computers and contemporary, child-focused literature. For them to have developed a similar obsession (as opposed, say, to a fixation on Harry Potter) is almost unimaginable.

The volume of *The Merry Adventures of Robin Hood* that formed my imagined world, written and illustrated by Howard Pyle in 1883, ends with the death of Robin. Unable, for some peculiar reason, to shoot his arrows straight, he goes to the prioress to be bled. But the prioress is a traitor to the merry men; she opens a vein in Robin's arm and bleeds him to death. With his last bit of energy, he shoots an arrow out of the priory window, and is buried where it comes to ground. In my mind, something about the sharp arrow and the horror of having a vein opened combined to make me hug both arms to my chest every time I thought about needles puncturing the walls of the bloodstream. I have never succeeded in giving blood. Death by injection is an ongoing fear.

But whereas a needle in a vein feels like a violation, a needle stroking its bloodless way through a design affords sensual pleasure. There's the way it enters the canvas, or the fabric, or the space between loops of yarn. The way it exits, trailing its twisted strand of wool or thread, making what has been punctured more secure, more solid and useful. Even the scar on the underside of my left arm, from surgery following a wrist break, was made by a needle pulling the sliced skin back together, making it whole.

If there was one aspect of life my mother craved despite her

                    Meditations for a New Century

denials, it was sensual pleasure. This, too, reports to historical circumstance. Her father came of solid Irish stock, but when he finally entered the hospital for the tuberculosis he had contracted in World War I, he weighed 106 pounds. He had waited too long. He was an up-and-comer who'd married a fair American girl of English descent and made his way in Chicago business. TB was considered a disease of the shanty Irish. Until he could scarcely stand on his feet any longer, the shame was too much to bear. In my mother's case, the disease lodged in the lymph nodes of her groin. Like her father, she was encouraged to eat and especially to drink milk, to fatten up, and she hated it. She was also on the edge of adolescence. One day, when she was scheduled to have one of the swollen nodes lanced, the doctor came through the ward on his rounds with a covey of medical students, all men. They gathered around the foot of my mother's cot.

"Now here's an interesting case," the doctor said.

He ordered the nurse to remove the covers from the cot and to lift up my mother's hospital gown. Then the nurse splayed apart my mother's thighs. The men leaned in. They stared. The doctor drew out his long needle. With bright light shining on my mother's preadolescent genitalia and a half-dozen men as witness, he punctured the swollen node while my mother screamed.

A few months later, her father died. Throughout their separate confinement, he had sent her letters—letters full of poetry and love, full of romance, calling her his little darling. Barred from his funeral, for a half-century she refused to weep. Then, in her early 60s, she woke sobbing from a dream of her father, and she sobbed all night. "It was like a flood," she told me. "I couldn't do anything to stop it."

When she'd finally emerged from the hospital, she knew two enemies: doctors who make you eat, and men who part your legs. For the rest of her life she disdained food and disliked sex. But in the middle of some nights, I could hear her in the kitchen gobbling caramels. She participated with alacrity in the cocktail culture of her time. And she wielded her needles with a deftness that approached genius. She made real Mary Lamb's arch admission that needlework "taken up as an amusement may not be altogether unamusing."

I look at the purse. That it came from my mother's hands; that it belonged to my mother; and that it belonged, and still belongs, uniquely to a moment in time and place when she was 36 years old in the Midwest of Dwight Eisenhower's America breaks my heart a little every time. It testifies to her urge, which is my urge and perhaps everyone's, to transcend —and it denies any transcendence. Though time never wore away its rich colors or sturdy wool stitching, my mother stopped using it in the 1970s. It was out of fashion by then. She had returned to work. A leather shoulder bag made much more sense. "Oh, that old thing," I can hear her saying. Though she never threw it away—it's hard to toss what your hands have crafted—she probably forgot it on the upper shelf of her closet.

We are not, in other words, fixed in time. I would not claim that the purse I regard so closely encapsulates my mother. She changed as she moved through history, each moment equally new and consequent of other moments. And then she stopped changing, because she stopped being. (The same thing happens to J.M. Barrie's Peter Pan, "dressed in skeleton leaves," who refuses to grow up. Barrie based Peter in part on his brother, dead at 13.) The needlepoint purse is a signifier of identity in time, but it is not identity. There's some relief in that. Still, if I'm to come to terms with my mother's immanence—no maternal soul out there watching over me—I have to admit my own. Something sparks me with terror. Am I not who I am because deep inside there's a consciousness for which the impersonal march of history is pure contingence? I'm governed by mortality, sure. But a mortality inextricable from this particular span? Isn't my membership, for instance, in the baby-boomer generation—with its easy answers, its sentimental nostalgia for the lyrics of Lennon's "Imagine," its cringeworthy ability to put oneself first—purely an accident?

No. Much as David Foster Wallace, in his famous address at Kenyon College, urged his young listeners to "consciously decide what has meaning and what doesn't," he wasn't about to tell them that all their decisions, all their goals, even all their regrets could only be theirs within the culture of the various moments in which they lived. However wide or deep their imaginations, they would fail, like Woody Allen's hero in *Midnight in Paris*, if they tried to create their lives' meaning according to different historical parameters.

Finally, if we seal ourselves to history when we die, our deaths seal history to us. If humans were immortal, maybe there would be no history to speak of, no world that could only be this world, now—any more than we in it could be ourselves. We refer to prehistory as the time before written records. It may be that those records—whether they constitute marks on paper or notches on stick or stone—create time, and in so doing create the very mechanism that defines us as individuals.

My children, when I die, will throw that needlepoint purse away. It holds no meaning for them. What will, for them, constitute the stone out of whose pond-ripples my life extended to the shores of my time is past my imagining. Whatever little thing they might choose, like my fixing on the purse, will from my point of view be insufficient, will be wrong. Or would be. Because I will be dead. And only the living, while they live in their time, think they have an argument to make.

Meditation on Stamps

A few decades ago, I received two letters from my father. The first had been re-sent after the post office returned it to him for insufficient postage. As in most of his letters, my dad spent his energy commenting on whatever I had written to him in my previous letter. If I told him, for instance, that I was dropping a class in physical anthropology and adding one in astronomy, he would begin with "You wrote on September 5 that," followed by a direct quote, followed by his opinion on anthropology and astronomy. Finally, he would close with a paragraph on what he and Nancy, my stepmother, were doing— usually church activities, sometimes outings with "our good friends, the Petersons," occasionally a meeting of the local Council on World Affairs or a new case he was considering as a circuit judge.

In the second letter, which arrived the same day, my father expressed his pique at the postal service. A week earlier, bearing an envelope with an old stamp that was one cent short of the new price, he arrived at the post office a few minutes after the doors had closed. (My father was habitually late, a trait my mother chalked up to narcissism.) He had seen employees inside but when he knocked on the door, they had turned their backs. Back home, he carefully taped a penny to the envelope, then he returned and dropped it into the mailbox for 7 a.m. pickup. Its return to him the next day had horrified him. He could not understand why a postal employee would not see the good sense of replacing his penny with a penny stamp.

I smirked at my father's naiveté. I had no idea how letters were sorted, but if employees were involved, I was certain they worked in some environment completely separate from the kindly clerk at the window. They had no drawer in front of them replete with penny stamps. His frustration over the returned letter adhered to his nostalgia for nickel beers at the ballpark and the ubiquity of hats.

My father died eighteen years ago, six days after my mother's death.[1] From him I received about a hundred so-called collectible coins and the Time/Life set of classical LPs he had garnered by subscription over ten years.[2] Not long ago, clearing out cabinets, my stepmother sent me more of my inheritance: two large FedEx boxes filled with objects she thought I, as what she labeled "the family historian," might wish to preserve. They sat for a long time on my study floor. When dust bunnies began to gather around the boxes, I started sorting. Some of the items were automatic discards—the large, cheap plastic frame in which my father had inserted a color photograph of the two of us when I was thirty and he seventy-two; the leather binder awarded him by Blue Cross Hospital Service; the funeral guestbook filled with names of people now mostly dead; my father's longhand records of the proceedings of the St. Louis Republican Committee. What remained were oxidized manila folders filled with documents. My father first ran for a St. Louis County judgeship on a Republican ticket in 1954, the year of my birth. He saved voluminous correspondence and lists from the Committee to Elect Franklin Ferriss. He saved hundreds of yellowing newspaper clippings. He saved letters of support; he saved letters of congratulation when he won. Other folders contained further letters from well-wishers over the years, as he ran for office four times on a party ticket and then at last without political affiliation. As a small-town politician and an active member of his congregation, my father was also a committed philanthropist, and a very fat folder holds letters of solidarity or thanks from hundreds of fellow philanthropists,

---

[1] The reaction most people had when they learned the news at the time was to invoke the shared lives and deaths of those long married. I flummoxed them by pointing out that my parents had been divorced, by then, for two decades. I added to the snark by quipping that my father, eleven years older than my mom but a nonsmoker and aficionado of Army calisthenics, had always sworn he would outlive her. The fact was that her death struck him to the core, and he had no trouble, the day of her funeral, in giving up his own ghost.

[2] These LPs, in their elegant boxes, mounted from floor to ceiling. I lived a thousand miles away. I gave them, along with the phonograph and speakers, to the county prison, where the person on the phone assured me that the inmates loved music.

committee chairs, board members, and recipients of generosity.

Some of these letters, mostly those by women, are written longhand, in the cursive so vigorously taught in the first half of the twentieth century. Others—almost entirely from men—are typed, probably originally dictated to a secretary or even written by a secretary sufficiently versed in her boss's way of expressing thanks. Some are on stationery, some on notecards, some on lined or unlined paper. All of them were folded and tucked into an envelope on which an address and return address were written and a stamp affixed before sealing and taking to a mailbox or the post office for delivery.

I cannot keep all these letters. I don't know why I am the keeper of anything, really. My basement is damp; twice it has flooded, despite new drains around the perimeter and an alarm tied into the security system. All summer we run a dehumidifier, but none of the boxes tucked on the shelves are properly wrapped or protected against mold. The boxes contain hundreds of old photographs of unidentifiable people who were vibrantly alive in the 1940s. They contain my great-great-grandfather's account of guarding the White House toward the end of the Civil War. My mother's "autobiography," written for a school assignment when she was ten, in which she includes as an addendum, "I forgot to tell you that my father died when I was 9 years old." Invitations to grand balls held at the end of the nineteenth century. Who will want all this stuff when I'm gone? Who will go through it? If we had such things from some family archive stretching back to the Wars of the Roses, we might find an astonishing image, a surprise story, a taste of the moment unavailable in history books. We would also need to train ourselves in deciphering the handwriting of 1550. Today, my students born at the millennium cannot read the marginalia I write in my Palmer cursive. I cannot read my maternal grandmother's shorthand, written in a style that was discarded around 1940. History matures into runes.

I need, then, to reduce the bulk of the material my stepmother has sent. If I don't do it now, no one will in future. If they have a large storage space, they will dump everything there and then toss it when they run short of room. But a small box, well-labeled, stands a chance of survival, at least for another generation.

I do not find any love letters from my mother, though I know she wrote them: The material from her closet, already stored downstairs on the shelves, includes letters from my dad that reference hers. Perhaps he or my stepmother destroyed them. Remaining are a handful of the hundreds of letters I wrote home after I moved away at age seventeen. Most of these were presumably not considered noteworthy, though the ones in the files are heavily outlined and annotated by my father in preparation for his replies.

Instead, I thumb through the enormous folder labeled "Complimentary letters." The stamps range from 3 cents to 32 cents over more than three decades. They express thanks in ways that are almost unimaginable today, even via the comparatively finger-snap mode of email. This, handwritten on personalized stationery, from a woman whose adoption apparently went through my father's courtroom: *Just a note to thank you for your wonderful help to us, throughout the adoption particulars. And many thanks, too, for your kind description to Johnny, about his new name. Both Bud and I appreciate your kindness very much. Most sincerely.* This, also handwritten, with a 3-cent stamp from 1957: *I am returning the pamphlet that I inadvertently took from the jurors' room last week. This was my first time to serve as a juror and I'm glad of this opportunity to express my deep appreciation of the way you explain things to new jurors. I'm sure many men there last week felt the same as I did. So, thanks from us, and keep up the good work. Sincerely.*

As the price of stamps goes up, the senders tack on 1-cent stamps until they've used up their old supply. I don't know if any of these stamps are collectible. The post office still encourages the collecting of stamps. Like the makers of the inherited coins that litter my bottom drawer, the postal service seems to come out with new images purely to sell them to collectors. The stamps on these envelopes—my father almost invariably saved the envelope, presumably for the return address—were licked by grateful newlyweds, grateful divorcés and divorcées and their lawyers, grateful students and teachers who visited the courtroom, grateful professionals who had received letters of congratulation from my father and wrote back with their thanks, grateful convicted criminals, grateful alcoholics, grateful churchgoers (my dad was deeply religious), grateful charities. My father generally wrote "Here's a keeper!" on the envelope before he tucked it into the folder. Often, he wrote back, and the carbon copies of his response are signed in ink and clipped to the original thank-you notes. I will keep almost none of these, with the exception of a couple of notes from my father's siblings

                    Meditations for a New Century

whose children are alive and may want these letters; and a letter from my grandfather congratulating my dad on his election. This last is notable because my grandparents lived four miles away and saw my parents almost every Sunday for dinner. Apparently the protocol was such that to congratulate your son, you sat down with nubbled paper, penned something relatively formal, signed it "Your loving Father," addressed the envelope, found and licked and pasted the stamp, and dropped it into the mailbox.

Another folder is labeled "Congratulations." Of these "keepers," I keep only two. One is from my father's opponent in the Republican primary, who was also a precinct chair. With his congratulations he encloses a sample ballot, printed on pinkish newsprint, where he has hand-totaled the ballots cast for both Republicans and Democrats,[3] showing my father's close win in an otherwise Democratic district. The other came from my great-uncle, Hugh Ferriss, a prominent New York architect whom I remember as a gruff presence with an oversized head of silvery hair and a bushy mustache. Uncle Hugh is famous enough that his work hangs in the Museum of Modern Art; perhaps there's some microscopic historical value to his apology for tardiness—"I have just finished a rather grueling job which has run over the past six weeks"[4]—and his noting that he had actually splurged on a station-to-station phone call only to learn from the "maid" that the victory party was elsewhere.

An envelope delivered without a stamp was even more precious than one with a stamp: These missives had been delivered by hand. Such was the case with invitations to formal balls. To send such things through ordinary mail was an affront. Anyone could receive a letter paid for by a stamp, an envelope that had passed through the public space of the postal system. Hand delivery was

———————————————

[3] Indicated by a Statue of Liberty rather than a donkey, though the Republicans stuck with their elephant. I've been unable to find a source for this symbol; everyone seems to think the donkey's been the go-to mascot for the Dems ever since Thomas Nast drew one in the early nineteenth century. Since the sample ballot was produced by the Republican Party, maybe they thought the statue looked less appealing than the jackass.

[4] Probably the initial sketches for Lincoln Center.

personal and private. The sender had paid for a human being, not a stamp, to deliver the message.

I didn't think about the obvious fact that stamps pay for mail delivery until recently, when a group of us with cottages on an unmanaged network of private dirt roads in the Berkshires began trying to renovate our dilapidated set of mailboxes, just off the state highway. We had to investigate who owned the land the mailboxes sat on, who owned the boxes themselves, whether we who could claim no boxes had to pay for a box at the post office. I learned, then, that as the resident of a legal address, I am entitled to free mail delivery. The stamps on the letters pay for the service.

It was not always so. Before 1840—a blink in time!—the recipient of a letter or package paid its delivery cost. Anyone who grew up with collect long-distance phone calls knows how this works.[5] You arranged some sort of code, visible on the outside of the letter (no envelopes, then), which the recipient scanned quickly to get the message you meant to deliver. Then the recipient refused delivery, just as the parents of the twentieth century refused the collect call and then direct-dialed their kid back, saving the operator's fees. Since mail carriers made their living off the payment they received after hauling

———————————————

[5] When I was in college, I took a summer job at a pastry shop outside Paris and spent my earnings on a moped, a crossover between bicycle and motorcycle. Riding this contraption north to the Edinburgh Festival of the Arts, I managed to earn college credit attending a lecture in the morning and the festival for the rest of the day. Afterward, I rode across the Scottish lake country, westward on the ferry, through the war zone of Northern Ireland (this was an accident; I hadn't been reading the news), and finally south to Cork, where my mother's family originated. The moped did not run in the rain, which was constant, and I had a cut on my right ring finger that swelled. I would stop at pubs while it poured, but many did not allow women past the tiny lobby. My mother in St. Louis, who thought me mad, had told me that if the going got too rough, I could call her collect. Standing in a vestibule in Donegal, watching the rain sheet down, my finger throbbing, cold, hungry, lonely, I lifted the receiver from its cradle on the pay phone and asked the operator to place the call. "I'll call ye back, dear," she said. I replaced the receiver. I waited. The rain lifted; the clouds cleared. After twenty minutes, the phone rang. "All circuits across the Atlantic are busy now, dear," the operator said. I hung up, went out, wiped off my wet seat, and rode on.

the mail over mountain, river, and hostile territory (and sometimes earned a little extra for spying on the contents of their cargo), the system broke down. Enter Rowland Hill, a British educator and advocate for the colonization of Australia, among other new-fangled ideas. He proposed what became the Penny Black, a small adhesive square featuring a young Queen Victoria's profile. That the idea was initially dismissed as "wild" and "preposterous" tells you all you need to know about the limits of legislators' imaginations. And that a mint Penny Black today fetches $3,000 at auction suggests how all this stamp-collecting business began.

In "Game of Thrones," that most violent and most nostalgic of all big-budget television enterprises, correspondence is delivered by raven. There's an almost laughable simulated caw that attends delivery and that comedian Stephen Colbert has made use of in his monologues. What sort of system creates these remarkable recipient-seeking ravens, whose expertise and reliability easily trump the USPS, is unclear. Despite the emphasis on freeing slaves in the series, the ravens, like Danaerys Targaryen's dragons, provide consistent unpaid labor. I assume that George R.R. Martin and the producers of the series chose ravens for airmail because carrier pigeons lacked the caw, the quick wit, and the dark profile of ravens. But if they had dug just a little, they would have found that even pigeon post called for stamps. The pigeons themselves may have been birds of burden, but someone had to feed them, train them, transport them from their home (that's how they knew where to go—their compass pointed toward home, so for the most part we're talking one-way trips), and attach those tiny letters to their tiny legs. Hence, stamps.

There were—and are—plenty of stamps other than postage, of course. Eagle stamps, for instance, which my mother, like every mother in St. Louis, collected. She filled her little booklet with them, and then she went to the redemption store in North County, where almost nothing from the catalog was actually on the shelves. I preferred Site stamps, which came only from the gas station on Lindbergh Boulevard, where I begged my mom or dad to stop so I could grab a dozen stamps to paste in my own booklet. Site had a catalog. For my mother's birthday one year, I sent off my entire trove of stamps and presented her with a fancy filigreed wastebasket to place next to the desk where she paid bills. It seemed like magic to me, turning the taste of that fine sheen of glue into the biggest present I had ever given anyone.

On the other hand, licking stamps made my tongue ache, and there was always the possibility of slicing my tongue when I licked the envelope flap. Today, on the rare occasion when I have to go through the rigmarole of finding the envelope (the flap now stuck to the body from sitting in a humid pigeonhole), finding the Human Rights Watch return label, finding a working pen for the address, finding the roll of Forever stamps I bought five years ago, and finding a mailbox (every week, it seems, one disappears), I hate the whole business. Even the Forever stamps—think about it. Yes, people used to keep a cache of penny stamps to plaster every time the P.O. raised the rates. My father's outrage over his taped penny would have been solved with a Forever stamp. But this way, the postal service gets the float, while we get rolls of stamps gradually drying out in a forgotten drawer.

Remember the float?

But no, that's banks. Checks that you wrote over your balance, holding your breath, hoping your paycheck would come in before the company in Texas received your check in the mail, deposited it, and had it cleared by the Texas bank. With the float came the risk of the bounce. You dated your checks April 30 and mailed them on May 2, hoping that the receiver wouldn't notice the postmark over the stamp. No one wants to return to those days.

The very word, *stamp*, comes not from the sticky squares but from the idea of pressing a seal or signature onto a document, verifying it. Today, our emails are timestamped. In 1954, the congratulations that flooded my father's mail when he first won his judgeship included several dozen telegrams, which were hand-delivered but nonetheless franked by place, date, and time, on paper now the color of marzipan. The messages themselves run in light violet all caps on strips that have been carefully glued onto the sheet. *Stampare* in Italian means "to print." For a Halloween party in the BI (Before Internet) era, I pinned stray pages of poetry and fiction to my clothes and went to the post office, where I asked the clerk to stamp me Return to Sender. "I can't do that," said the clerk, as if this were a routine pesky request.

"But I'm attending a party as an unsolicited manuscript," I said.

"We're not allowed to stamp people, only envelopes."

"Is that the stamp?" I pointed to a block next to a red ink pad.

     Meditations for a New Century

The clerk nodded. "Can you turn your back just a second?" I asked.

He was a nice guy. I stamped Return to Sender and Wrong Address all over my face and hands. To thank the guy, I bought a roll of stamps as well, and wore them as a necklace. I suspect they had flags on them, as if something patriotic attended their deployment, but I lost them at the party anyway.

In Europe, now, the stamps you purchase, white rectangles with requisite information about cost, date, and origin, come from a self-serve machine with no potential for nostalgia. In other words, the image launched by the Penny Black, of a stamp as a small sticky square with a meaningful image, may prove a two-hundred-year fleeting moment.

But America is a land of nostalgia. When the usefulness of an object exits the stage, skeuomorphism enters. Many of the features on our computer screen are carefully constructed skeuomorphs—the "raised leather stitching" on our Address Book, the old-fashioned video camera of FaceTime, the "folders" by which we organize our documents. (We also paste vinyl strips onto our windows to simulate mullions, and slap "wood-grained" vinyl onto the sides of our cars.) The envelopes holding presorted first-class pleas for donations and memberships, I've begun to notice, are stamped—or appear to be stamped—the old-fashioned way. But when I look closely, I see that the so-called stamps are carefully printed on the envelope itself. Using trompe l'oeil, the stamps appear to sit on top of the paper. Sometimes they are deliberately skewed to simulate a human being's sloppy placement. Other times, they include two or three images of stamps as if the sender never heard of Forever stamps and had to add up the postage herself:

I'm ridiculously curious about the effect of this maneuver.

With the possible, and vanishing, exception of Christmas cards, actual correspondence is not what I expect from the mail carrier, and the skeuomorphic stamps don't fool me into thinking a human being has found some peculiar reason to write to me. And yet it does take longer for these pieces of mail to slide into the recycle bin. I do occasionally open one of these envelopes in preference to the envelopes with the stampless postmark. I assume this response is the same reason other simulacra[6] abound—because nostalgia is rooted somewhere in our lizard brains and not at the rational level.

I'm still working through the small, neat box, labeled *F Ferriss correspondence*, which I'll leave for some possible future historian. By the time it's opened, only the context of the messages will be of importance, not the identity of the man who clipped a penny to an envelope and assumed it would reach its destination. The only place that identity, and the identities of the hundreds of ghosts who haunt these yellowing folders, might have remained would be on the stamps, where a scientist could potentially extract from the glue a trace of DNA. Maybe a different family historian would hang onto the stamps in case they're worth money one day. I hesitate, then slide the stamped envelopes into the recycle bin. Sometimes, *pace* Faulkner, the past is past.

---

[6] The simulacrum is related to the skeuomorph, and I take sensual pleasure in saying both words aloud. The French philosopher Jean Baudrillard was the one who nailed the simulacrum as being not just a representation of something, but a representation for which there no longer is, or never was, an original. "The map," he writes, "engenders the territory." My favorite example of simulacra is the "most photographed barn in America" in Don Delillo's *White Noise*. "Once you've seen the signs about the barn," says a character named Murray, "it becomes impossible to see the barn." The same may become true of stamps.

Meditation on Middle G

My musical friends tell me there's no such thing. There's middle C, they say. Anything else is just G. G above middle C, G below middle C, high G. I think of the note as middle G, though, and I cannot sing it. It's in what they call my "break," the place where chest voice shifts into head voice. Singing like a soprano, I emit a breathy sound, as if the only muscles I can summon to push out the note bunch around my throat and clavicle. Slipping into a tenorish chest voice, I force the sound up from my belly through my adenoids until a headache shoots from the top of my palate through my scalp.

Most songs, at least for women, include middle G. It's the tonic of the C scale, the dominant of the G, the minor seventh of the A. It's the note you're supposed to belt out, if you're belting. It's where a singer is meant to feel happiest. If I were to draw middle G, it would look something like this:

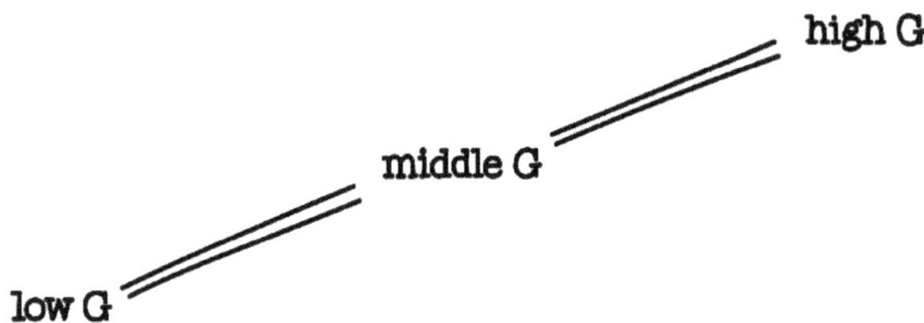

I've been singing all my life. My voice has no character, but most days I don't care. I can read music, I can hit the notes, I remember most of the words, and I cheer up when I sing. Only middle G lurks inside me like a secret wound, the simple moment that grows vexed whenever I try to locate it.

Make B's, my mother said. This was when B's were good grades.

Decent grades, you called them. Parents weren't ashamed of daughters who made B's. More to the point, they had a shot at popularity. Girls were meant to be well-liked. How hard was it, to be liked, if you wore more or less the right clothes, told more or less the right jokes, smiled a lot? B's were middle G. Being well-liked was middle G. I couldn't manage it.

I had skipped fifth grade. This is sheer numerical coincidence, but middle G is the fifth note of the C scale. In fifth grade, most girls turn 11 and enter the first stages of puberty.[7] Fifth grade is the break. Skipping it at a girls-only school, I acquired the reputation of the Smart Girl, or the Girl Who Thought She Was Smart. While other girls popped breasts like bread rising overnight, my chest remained stubbornly flat, my pudenda embarrassingly smooth. If I failed to make A's, I would be exposed as a fraud. If I made them, my label would stick to me like reptile scales. My sixth-grade teacher, Mrs. Woolcott, fiercely resented the problem I posed. In the first few weeks of school, I kept forgetting we had homework. There hadn't been homework in fourth grade, and neither of my parents seemed to realize that I was supposed to fill out worksheets and complete math problems in the evenings. First thing in the mornings, the school held chapel, and while the girls bowed their heads to say the school prayer—*Watch over our school, O Lord, as its years increase, and bless and guide its daughters, wherever they may be, keeping them ever unspotted from the world*—I generally remembered the homework I should have done the night before. I filed back to the classroom sick at heart.

Sometime in that first month, on the way out of Chapel and just before Spelling, I told Mrs. Woolcott that I felt ill. While I was hiding in the small, dark room behind the nurse's office, where three cots lined up with their thin waffle blankets, Mrs. Woolcott told one of the other sixth-graders to open my desk. She pulled out my spelling exercise book, its pages for that day splendidly unmarked, and passed it around, demonstrating to my new, breast-budding classmates that I was a fraud.

Make B's, my mother said. Hide your lamp under a bushel.[8]

———————————————————————

[7] At least in the 1960s; it comes earlier, now

[8] This is a misquote from the Bible. In Luke 11:33, the King James version

I tried. But it hurt my heart to spell words wrong, so when I recovered from my shame and began completing the homework, I started getting A's in spelling. Latin was harder, thus easier to aim at a B. But my Latin teacher, Miss Pruitt, who liked to call us girls Petunias when she was angry,[9] would drag me into the corridor when it was time to hand out midterm grades. "Petunia," she said, "you are so smart. Why are you so stupid?"

I didn't know, I told her. I tried to smile. Maybe, I said, I wasn't that good at Latin.

"You have earned a B," she said. "But you should have earned an A. So I am giving you a C."

The same held true for clothes. That we couldn't afford the brands the other girls wore (Pappagallo, Honeybee, Lilly Pulitzer) wasn't the problem. That my sewing skills had been honed on my mother's 1900-vintage Wilcox & Gibbs chain-stitch machine wasn't the problem. The problem was, once I'd found the fabric and the pattern to match the social vibe at school, I went too far or not far enough. I wasn't content with buying fabric that looked sort of tie-dyed; I had to tie-dye it myself, in colors no one had seen at the store. My polka-dot minidress sported polka dots the size of pancakes. My high-waist bolero pants rose higher than everyone else's. Or else they failed to rise at all, or I neglected to put enough pin pleats into my pin-pleated shirtwaist, or the dots, too tiny now, echoed the flocked blouse our French teacher wore. I couldn't find the median. Middle G, in school, looked something like this:

reads, "No man, when he has lighted a lamp, puts it in a secret place, neither under a bushel, but on a lampstand, that they who come in may see the light." *Bushel* was apparently a mistranslation of the Aramaic word for *bowl*. Nonetheless, it did occur to me, every time my mother proffered this odd advice, that a lamp underneath a bushel, say, of hay, would start a fire.

[9] She claimed petunias stank. Apparently this is true only when they are thrown off their natural circadian rhythms by artificial light or altered genes; in their natural state, petunias emit a heady scent at night, to attract the hawk moths that pollinate them. Miss Pruitt, one suspects, kept a large window garden, brightly lit, and the flowers went haywire.

A's : flamboyant clothes; drinking too much; embarassing passions

B's, etc.

C's : dowdy clothes; not drinking; caring about nothing

"You were insecure," my husband says. "Everyone was insecure."

"Why would you want to be mediocre?" my best friend asks.

No one wants to be mediocre. In middle G, I want to say, lies genius. When I was very young, I thought I would be a tightrope walker. I spent hours walking my mother's garden fence, which was a six-inch tall border of metal rickrack. I tried to keep my gaze focused ahead, on the knot in the pine tree or the neighbor's back door. But I never made it to the end of the garden. My center of gravity was too high, my mother told me, and I wondered how she knew. Were we born that way, in our family? Or was my center of gravity a mistake I kept making? For me on the garden border, middle G looked like this:

I am the middle child in my family. When people learn my sibling position, they adopt a knowing look. "Middle child," they say. "We get it." The middle child is supposed to be the peacemaker, the socially adept one. But I never understood myself as being in the middle. I was my brother's competitive almost-twin; I was my adorable sister's bossy, resentful elder. I couldn't rest in the middle. It wasn't my place.

It's easy, and not entirely wrong, to conflate middle G with something we might call "normal." My college students talk about writing a "normal story" or a "normal essay." The defining characteristic of these mythical endeavors is their "relatability." A normal essay begins with a solid statement, marshals evidence, and presents a synthesizing conclusion. A normal story engages two or three characters in a conflict that builds to a dramatic scene and then resolves. Key to these normalcies is their kind indulgence of the reader's limits. The essay's premise can be fished up from the pond of received opinion. The story's characters are members of a group who wrestle with interpersonal crises. They are not spermatozoids. They do not shift from a bedroom in Manhattan to an outer, nameless wasteland. Slavering dogs do not appear throughout the narrative without connecting directly to the plot.

I once had a poetry teacher, a brilliant man, whose wife wrote verses for Hallmark greeting cards. They were hard up for cash, and she had more work than she could handle. She persuaded her boss to take on her poet-husband. He tried with all his might to write a Hallmark greeting card. He did not despise the form or the audience. He wanted the money. But he was a failure at it and got himself fired within a few weeks.

The stories my students want to write and the poetry my teacher tried hard to compose fall within certain boundaries:

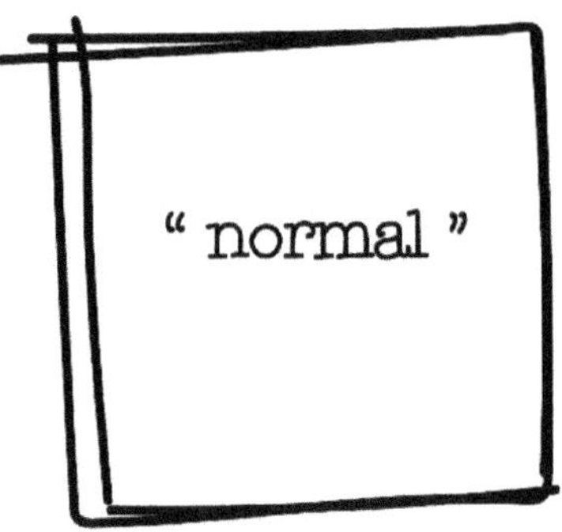

These norms are imposed from the outside. They are things to which we conform or—recklessly, brilliantly, or because we have no choice—fail to conform. Yet when Donald Trump was president of the United States, I cried out like everyone else I know, "This is not normal!" I didn't mean Donald Trump was failing to conform. I meant that I was terrified. I meant the situation was *abnormal*.

And no, gentle reader, there is no upside to abnormal. No free spirit, no maverick, no genius. No one yearns for abnormality. Normal, in this sense, is not a midpoint or a box, but one side of a divide:

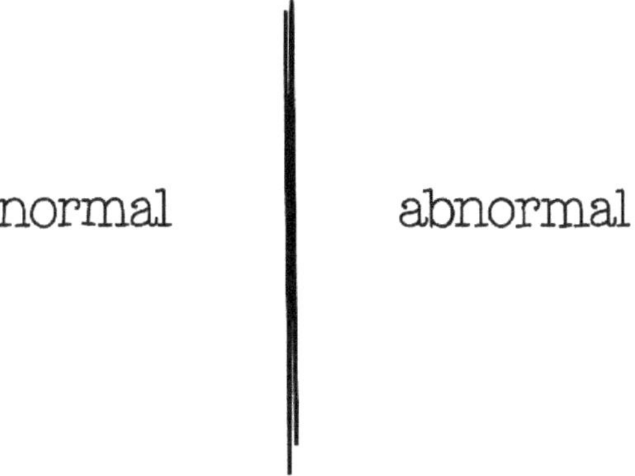

There's no middle ground here. There's sickness and health, kind and cruel. You want one of those, not the other. You have no longing to fall somewhere halfway between. For the politics of the twenty-first century, middle G is a Trojan horse. Allowed within the gates under the guise of compromise, it will open its belly to the murderous fantasies of QAnon.

Religious traditions—the older ones, not today's evangelicals—cultivate the idea of a center. The Shakers sing it:

'Tis a gift to be simple, 'tis a gift to be free.

'Tis a gift to come down where we ought to be

And when we find ourselves in the place just right

It will be in the valley of love and delight.

Quakers meet in a circle or a square, focusing their attention inward. "For the Quaker seesaw, the important point is the fulcrum," according to the 2007 Friends General Conference. "The individual and the meeting are in balance in relation to each other because of their relation to God, the Center, the Fulcrum."

Here, then, is the seesaw, balanced by middle G:

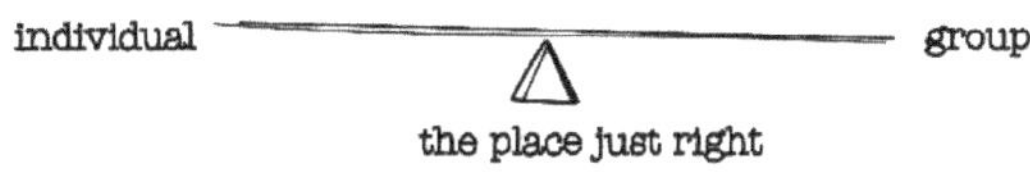

Various Eastern philosophies put a third eye in the center of the forehead. In Hinduism, the chakra leads to a higher plane of consciousness. In Taoism, the third eye opens up inside the forehead and creates a space between the body's two hemispheres. In

Buddhism, it symbolizes the mind's eye, the perfect center where so-called reality vanishes into insubstantiality.

For the past four years, I've been meditating. What I've chosen is the McDonald's of meditation: an app on my iPhone, in which a sexy British guy named Andy Puddicombe guides me through breathing and imaging protocols completely devoid of any reference to spirits or enlightenment. My goal is lower blood pressure. Not that I have high blood pressure, but I get anxious just thinking about the circulation of the blood, and so I am a poster child for what's known as white-coat syndrome, in which taking your blood pressure makes your blood pressure rise.[10]

For decades, I resisted any call to meditation-qua-meditation. I swam; I counted laps. The real reason for my resistance was my brief marriage, in my early twenties, to an avowed Zen Buddhist who looked like the Marlboro Man and who provided cover for me from my sexually predatory employer. We don't need to get into that story.[11] The point here is that the marriage quickly went south. I thought we needed counseling; the Zen Buddhist thought I needed to find my center. I agreed to try things his way if he would try things my way. For a month, I meditated daily for twenty minutes. I studied my breathing. I counted to ten, then began again at one. Nothing else in our pallid, distant relationship changed, and he still refused to seek counseling. So I stopped meditating and divorced him.

On one other occasion, I had tried to locate my center. This was at the Mount Baldy Zen Center in California. I cannot remember how I found myself there, but it was with a group of inquiring minds. Monks, residents, and guests took their places on satin pillows in a wide, skylit room. We novices were given instructions. Those who could achieve the lotus position did so; the rest of us sat cross-legged and tried not to slump. We shut our eyes and kept silence for a long

---

[10] Case in point: While writing this, I realized I hadn't taken my blood pressure for a while. I strapped on the cuff but felt the heat flowing into my face, so I surfed the Internet for a couple of minutes, then hit the button casually, as if my life didn't depend on these numbers. The result: 112/80. I recorded it in the health app on my phone. My phone contains my life.

[11] See above, in discussion of "normal."

while, until a gong sounded. During that time, something happened to me. If I had to name it, I would call it middle G. That is, I felt myself for a long moment suspended in time and space, perfectly balanced, as if God or someone held me in the palm of his hand. My head seemed to lift from my shoulders and float.

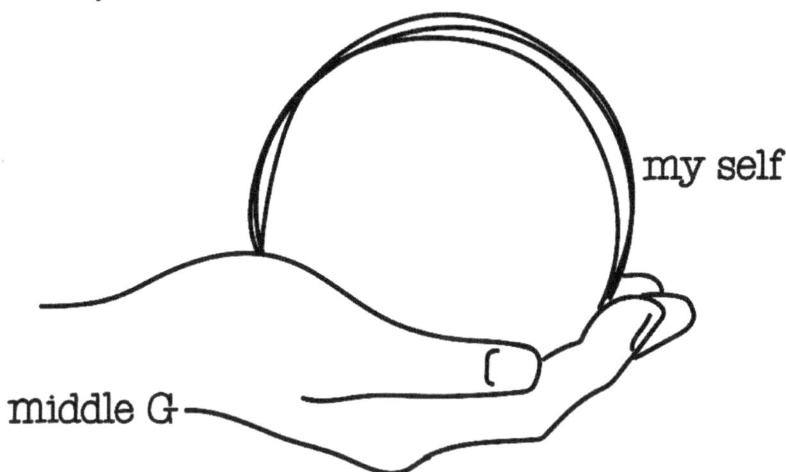

It was a deeply pleasurable and frightening sensation, not unlike my first orgasm, when the pleasure that washed over me filled me at once with joy at its presence and panic that the gates to this heaven would shut and I would never know how I found the combination in the first place. When the gong sounded and we opened our eyes, I experienced a Tilt-A-Whirl vertigo, as if I might tumble from my satin pillow. Afterward, while others walked through the green gardens, I went to visit the Roshi. I told him of my experience. What might I do, I asked, to further explore this state of being?

"I will not answer you," he told me.

But I wanted to know, I said. I wanted to learn.

He shrugged. He could not give me advice. Everything, he said, was up to me.

"I fucking hate Buddhists," I said in the van on the way down. My comrades looked aghast. My eyes and throat burned, tears wanting out.

In this iteration, middle G constructs a balance point, smaller than a pinpoint, that opens a space inside. The desire for that transcendent center seems not to intersect with the desire to be average. There's a certain gendered aspect to this distinction. Girls everywhere learn to think of so-called balance as a meaningful life goal, to advance by persuasion rather than threat. It's not lost on me that my mother's notion of middle G consisted of tamping down genius, whereas men like the Zen Roshi or Andy Puddicombe propose centeredness as a mysterious achievement.

Maybe I'm making a category mistake. I learned about category mistakes in a college philosophy class.[12] Maybe it's not just that I'm putting, say, "making B's" in the same category with "singing middle G" and "achieving satori." Maybe what I'm after, with middle G, has the same contours as Ryle was outlining: that is, I am making a big mistake, from which all the little mistakes follow.

In my first full-time teaching job, my colleagues gave me a pamphlet with their policy on marking papers, which I was to follow. One expression we were to correct was "center around." Logically, the pamphlet pointed out, you could not center around something; you had to center on it. If you want to be going around a center, you could use the word *revolve*. But revolving implies a circular motion, in a direction. I have centered around things many times, I wanted to protest. Middle G is one of them. If I could center on it, I wouldn't be writing this meditation.

Instead, the search itself for middle G suffers, as it were, from an anxiety about middle G. To center on the center is to awaken fear. The great funambulist Philippe Petit has said that fear while on the wire is the most dangerous experience for a wire-walker.[13] It may be in the nature of a fulcrum that one cannot know one is on it, or close to being on it. "Did you ever wait for the longest day of the year and then miss it?" Daisy says in *The Great Gatsby.* And as Wordsworth

----

[12] Gilbert Ryle coined the term in 1949 to counter Descartes, who spent much energy distinguishing the brain from the mind. Ryle said Descartes was making "one big mistake and a mistake of a special kind. It is, namely, a category mistake. It represents the facts of mental life as if they belonged to one logical type or category . . . when they actually belong to another."

[13] "The wire is a safe place for me to be. The street is not. Life is not. It's a rigorous and simple path. It's straight. You don't have meanders like, you know, on the ground, in life."

climbs the Alps, searching and searching for the point where the rise will become the fall, he experiences this:

> A peasant met us, from whose mouth we learned
> That to the spot which had perplexed us first
> We must descend, and there should find the road,
> Which in the stony channel of the stream
> Lay a few steps, and then along its banks;
> And, that our future course, all plain to sight,
> Was downwards, with the current of that stream.
> Loth to believe what we so grieved to hear,
> For still we had hopes that pointed to the clouds,
> We questioned him again, and yet again;
> But every word that from the peasant's lips
> Came in reply, translated by our feelings,
> Ended in this,— 'that we had crossed the Alps.'

The disappointment lies not in failing to achieve the summit, but in failing to mark the achievement, as if the Alpine summit, like the longest day, requires our confirmation. But if Philippe Petit had focused on his own balance, a half-mile over the Financial District, one suspects he would have fallen.

Before the pandemic hit, I began voice lessons again. When I first took lessons, ten years ago, the teacher kept pushing me to higher and higher notes, which ran me out of breath. Other techniques I acquired through choral singing included big-belly breathing, bending my knees as the notes go higher, waving my right arm in a circle for the arpeggios, pretending I had a quarter pinched between my butt cheeks. None of these produced a beautiful sound, and none helped me master middle G.

Carol, my new instructor, was a slim, long-haired, plain-faced woman who wore peasant skirts. She told me to take a deep breath and sing the note she was playing on the console piano. Then she told me I was doing it all wrong. Coming around to where I faced her from the other side of the piano, she pressed her hands on my shoulders so they hunched a little. She told me to take about a third of the breath I thought I needed, but to push the breath down, down, down. "Like a piston," she kept saying. She made a fist and pushed it downward through the air. I needed to use my diaphragm, yes, but the diaphragm is not a muscle and has no sensation. If the lower abdomen swells, it means my organs are being pressed down and out. I shouldn't tighten my abdominal muscles, the way I'd been taught. "Think about it," Carol said. "When you lift something heavy, you tighten those muscles, and what comes out of your mouth? A constrained, exploded oof! You want the opposite when you're singing."

Carol sang a short series of notes, *do-re-mi-re-do*, on a bright *aah.* She held her hands lightly on my waist and abdomen as I imitated her. She placed her hands under my chin, on my larynx to see how it sat. She pulled my jaw down and pinched underneath it, to loosen its muscles and let my tongue flop. She had me hold the tip of my tongue between my thumb and forefinger as I voiced the notes, to be sure the tongue was relaxed, that only the back of it (which, like the diaphragm, I couldn't feel) was working. When drool ran down my chin, Carol gave me a tissue. She told me not to listen to myself; that what I heard was nothing like the voice the rest of the world heard.

I shut my eyes as I repeated the notes. I had never actually seen a piston in operation but I imagined a fat metallic bar with a wide stop at the bottom, pressing down to my ovaries. We think of breathing as a rise and a fall, but this was the opposite: a descent on the inhale, a release on the exhale, fall then rise. Every time we met, Carol ran a do-re-mi series first in my lower register and then in my upper register. "Don't mix the registers," she told me.

After some weeks, my high notes stopped warbling and going flat. My low notes felt silkier. Something undeniably erotic about Carol's cool hands on these parts of my body kept me coming back for more. She was rearranging my insides in ways that gave me both vertigo and pleasure.

Slowly, I improved. I got the piston idea; I stopped filling the cavities of my upper chest with air. Carol had me sing a song only on vowels, and we spent five minutes arguing about whether to pronounce *God* with *ah* or *awh.* As I improved, I began to imagine something I never told Carol, even as she pressed into my flesh at various places. I imagined that I was singing, not through my vocal cords and mouth but through my vagina. I pressed the air down, I let my mouth flop open, and the sound emerged from between my legs. I was giving birth to my voice. It emerged weak, incontinent, mewling, and pure. When I tried again, my jaw muscles tightened, just as they had when I gave birth to a real human child. That time, I squeezed the muscles in my face so much that by the next day the flesh around my eyes had grown puffy and bruised. Now I told myself that dropping my jaw would open my vagina, like a remote hinge. I pressed down insistently to round the notes into a robust baby. I could not have told you what the sound was like; I couldn't seem to hear it.

And middle G? At first, middle G felt like the innermost part of whatever gift I was trying to unlock. It peeked out now and then but couldn't seem to go where the other notes—the high and low—went. It was the heart of my singing, but a tiny mouse heart, and for a little while leaving it alone seemed an act of mercy.

Eventually, though, Carol explained to me: Every woman has a middle-G problem, because women, unlike men, have two voices. The point where the voices—the registers—cross might be G or F or A, but what's important is that the problematic note lies high in chest voice and low in head voice. If I'm singing in my lower register, I have to push the air down harder to reach the G, and by focusing my energy downward, I produce a round sound, headache-free. In my upper register, I will get nowhere by pushing harder but neither will the voice find its full strength. Instead, I need to run lightly through it, to push hard only as the tune rises to a place of soprano strength. The trick, then, is not middle G itself, but deciding on what note to switch registers. Middle G is not the middle at all. It is the top or the bottom:

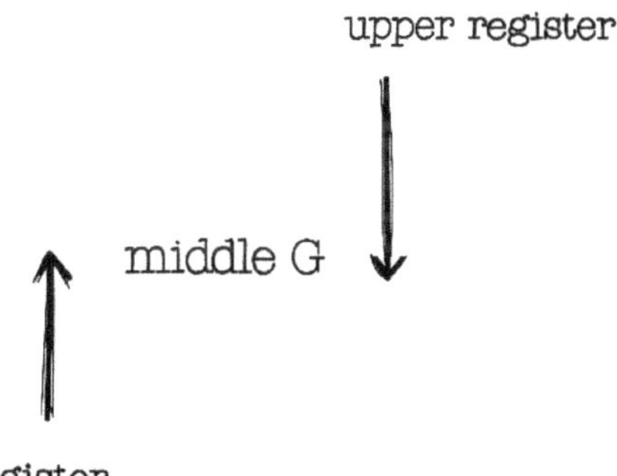

The metaphorical implications of thinking this through are almost painfully obvious, but I can't resist. Take what's called code-switching, shifting from one style or register of language to another. When the term first became popular, it was mostly in reference to Black Americans switching from street vernacular to formal English. But plenty of people in other groups, including white academics, code-switch. I'm fairly fond of casual profanity in my speech at home but in the classroom it disappears. When I was a young girl, I kept trying to find that exact note, that exact dialect and approach and attitude. I was trying to work within one female identity, one voice. I couldn't let the Smart Girl, for whom a B grade was a note too low to carry authority, rise into her strength. How astonishing to consider that in another register, where the Smart Girl had no place, my sartorial choices constituted the high note and took every bit of the panache I possessed. The adolescents around me might have seen one whole, indivisible individual, the way you will hear one song when I sing it. But I would have would have reached strong and hard for those tie dyes; I would have taken lightly the nexus of grades and popularity. *Don't mix the registers.*

When Andy Puddicombe speaks through my earbuds, he tells me to imagine my thoughts as a young wild horse gradually being tamed. He tells me to imagine the clear sky that always lies behind clouds of random associations. Or myself on an island, with the traffic of the world speeding around me. These are all fine images but at some point they cease to apply. The goal for which we're encouraged to strive—satori, the longest day, the midpoint of the wire—are mirages that vanish as you step inside them. To meditate, perhaps to worship, is to perform a search whose object is unknowable. The best result would be to reach the summit of the Alps without comprehending either *summit* or *Alps.*

Lately, I've shut Andy off. Closing my eyes, I picture the piston pressing down within me, pressing the beauty of my voice toward birth. Press, release. Press. Release. I don't know who I am as this happens. I don't know if I am normal. Having no sense of my limits, I define no central point. More registers sound within me than I can count. There is no middle G.

                    Meditations for a New Century

Meditation on Figure Drawing

We gather on Thursday nights. The barn housing us is said to be historic. It needs a new coat of paint, caulking for the windows, a roof that won't leak in the spring downpours, and better walls to hold in the woodstove heat with which we try to blast away the winter chill. The room needs to be warm, for the models. Naked, they hold their poses for up to forty minutes. A person can freeze to death in that time.

The only art training I ever received was in ninth grade, where I quickly fell behind the class during the unit on sculpture. The other students were welding metal while I still labored over my sandstone rabbit. By the time we got to charcoal and perspective, I understood that I lacked any natural affinity for form and representation. I needed more time than life would give me to learn what a shape was. I needed more of the steps broken down to render that shape on the page or in space. Only some alternate route toward learning would ever move me beyond stick figures. No such routes being available, I put the visual stuff away and built my raft of words.

A few years ago, however, I found myself at a retreat for writers and artists where figure drawing was offered, free, four mornings a week. Midway through my second week, the words a hopeless tangle, I escaped my studio. I stopped in at the tiny artists' supply shop on the premises. Too embarrassed to ask what I should equip myself with, I bought a sketch pad and a few sticks of charcoal and sneaked out, a spy in the house of art. I headed over to the barn. Inside sat a college kid reading a magazine on a sagging couch. He glanced up. "Someone at last," he said.

"Where are all the artists?" I said.

"Well, you're here," he said.

The visual artists had gotten bored, or weren't looking for a break from stacking orange juice cans or wiring some roadkill varmint to snap its jaws at the click of a switch. The kid started to undress. "What do you want me to do?" he asked.

"I don't know," I said. "I've never done this before."

"Usually I start with twenty-second poses. How's that?"

"Sure," I said. "Whatever you usually do."

Even to myself, I sounded suspiciously like a john at his first visit to a house of ill repute. The model was down to his jeans. He glanced over at me. He was a shortish young man, muscled through the chest, with just a whisper of beer belly. "If you get uncomfortable," he said, "I'm going to get uncomfortable."

"I'm not uncomfortable," I said. This was oddly true. The model was the age of my older son. "I'm just ignorant."

"Okay," he said. He pulled down his jeans and proceeded to stretch, first one way, then the other. Quickly I drew out my pad. I made lines—a spine, a hip, a shoulder and arm. The results looked Thurber-esque—though Thurber, I recalled as I squinted at my hapless cartoons, had had an excuse: He was almost blind.

"God, these are awful," I said.

"I'm sorry," said the model. "Am I moving too fast? Do you want a profile pose?"

"You're fine," I said.

"Maybe a long pose."

"Sure, that's good."

He settled onto the couch. At first I thought I ought to talk to him. We were the only people in the barn. In my experience, when a man and a woman are together, one of them unclothed, and they cease talking, they enter a dangerous realm. So I asked this young man what he was majoring in, how long he'd been modeling, which of the artists had sketched him, where his family lived. While he answered, I found my charcoal swirls gradually coming to focus on his leg. He was sitting now on the shabby couch, leaning back on a couple of pillows and propped on his arm. I could not imagine transferring his tilted body to the page or capturing the shadows that crossed his V-shaped torso from the barn's track lights. His body became amazing to me, a symphony of planes, angles, curves, dimples, hair. The leg on which my eyes settled was draped over the other leg, which was bent and tucked up on the couch and had the distinct disadvantage of possessing a foot in clear view. A foot! My god, how had anyone ever reproduced a foot?

I went from the hard charcoal to the soft. I broke a piece and turned it sideways to make shadows. There was the curve, yes, of the quad muscle as it spread over the dingy cushion. There was the tendon pulling on the knee. Gradually, as I made lines and erased them, abandoned one sheet of paper and started another, I realized that we had stopped talking. The model had picked up a book—Faulkner—and was reading. I didn't ask him about the book. I didn't want to know about the book. I only wanted to get that leg. Or maybe just the thigh. Just as far as the knee. The knee was a bitch. It was beautiful. There. And there. And there.

After forty-five minutes, I had had enough. I could not imagine anything I could do to improve my drawing of the leg. And the rest of the body intimidated me completely. I thanked the model and released him. "Man, this is the easiest gig," he said as he slipped his T-shirt on.

The rest of that day, I kept pulling out my drawing. I hated it for not being better. I remembered how long that sandstone rabbit took me, how I'd kept sanding away—under the ears, above the haunch—as if the sculpture were not being carved but somehow gestating under my hesitant fingers. Next day, I went back to the barn. This time there was one other artist, a Vietnamese painter who liked to execute wild abstracts in lacquer. She spoke just enough English to tell the college kid, with authority, where to stand, how to tilt his head, what to do with his feet. She worked with fat sticks of charcoal that looked nothing like what I'd found at the store. The figures on her page soon seemed to hold more life than the model himself. There was his pouch of fat, there his pectorals, there his chubby penis, there the straight narrow sweep of his nose, his vulnerable mouth.

I worked on another version of his leg. For more than an hour. It was better, though not by much. I did not want the painter to see it, and when she smiled at me I cringed at her condescension. Still, the rest of the day, I felt coursing through me the kind of energy I remembered from days playing sports in high school, those few times when I scored a goal. Something had happened. I had made it happen.

  Meditations for a New Century

The late John Updike, who spent a year at the Ruskin School of Art at the University of Oxford, spoke of "the itch to make dark marks on white paper" shared by writers and artists. That itch is no longer satisfied, in our computer age, by the act of writing. The fine muscles that once enabled Charles Dickens to compose dozens of pages by hand at a single sitting (and that may function still, in rare cases like that of J.K. Rowling, whose fans once deluged her with lined paper when she complained of running out) have gone lax and given way to carpal tunnel syndrome. My "writing itch," insofar as it applies to a physical event in real time with real ink on real paper, is meagerly satisfied by my pleasure in the loopy capitals *L* and *F* of my signature.

My first foray into figure drawing, then, may have stemmed from the urge to create, as William Gass put it, "words [that] would not be thought, they would be made." But figure drawing has appeal far beyond the tactile outlet denied by my computer. Writers down the ages have paid attention to what Gass dubbed "the dual muse." In his enormous compilation *The Writer's Brush*, Donald Friedman has gathered almost two hundred writer-artists, beginning with Johann Goethe and running through Jonathan Lethem. Going back further in time, no one would be surprised to learn that Plato sketched, or Chaucer. Lao-tze drew his characters as much as he wrote them.

Returned from my retreat to the ordinary rhythms of life, I have now joined a local figure-drawing circle. We meet once a week in an old barn converted to a community art league. The number of sketchers ranges from a half dozen to twenty. Most are men. A handful make a living teaching art; among the rest are a printer, a jeweler, an insurance salesman, several students, several unemployed. Most work in pencil or charcoal but some use India ink, pastels, watercolors. Our weekly contributions pay the professional models—some of them artists themselves—who pose for us.

I have gone from fearing the Thursday nights when we gather—Will I keep my focus? Will my drawing be too embarrassing?—to anticipating them with a sort of hunger. My compulsion to return every week, take up charcoal, and try to channel the human form from its living incarnation to the pebbly white of my sketch pad resembles the other sketchers', but it partakes also of my needs as a writer, and those needs themselves are no doubt unique to each writer who makes the attempt to draw or paint. In my case, I can articulate two distinct allures that the charmed Thursday circle represents for me. The first is an escape from the world of words; the second a return to it.

I tend to arrive at the barn late, after the model has begun her short poses and most of the easels are set up. The others nod and smile at me. If the circle is crowded, they make room. Someone's brought speakers for their iPhone, and folk music plays in the background. Logs crackle in the wood stove. Otherwise, the only sound is the susurrus of soft charcoal across paper. The model's skin, lit by the track lamps, always startles me. The pearliness of the young white woman with her dyed black hair. The milk coffee of the young Black woman. The ivory of the older man, and his bluish veins. So much skin. Where there is body hair, so much hair. To set myself up I fetch an easel from the wing of the barn that still has empty horse stalls. The model stands with her weight on one leg, arm lifted to the rafter, head thrown back. I get in a few lines, a shadow; then she shifts. She crouches with her back to me, huddled as if in fear. I try for the line of vertebrae, the back of the head, the curve of a buttock. Now she bends and reaches out, as if grabbing a child back from the edge of a cliff. My arm is moving in circles now, getting the rounded muscle of the shoulder, the loop of skin over the hip, the breast pulled one way by the outstretched arm and the other by gravity. I flip the pages of my drawing pad—I've learned to bring two pads, one for the quick poses, the other for the long pose—and work to keep up, to catch a bit of this body before it morphs. Others are working in miniature, fitting several sketches onto one page, but I cannot draw small.

"I'm taking a break," says the model.

She relaxes. Most of us put down our pencils, our charcoals, our pens. Some continue shading, extending, drawing already from memory. The model shrugs on a robe. Bill, the printer, steps into the kitchen to make coffee. We pull out our $15 donations. We clear our throats. Nancy asks Dave about his

  Meditations for a New Century

trip to New York. Marc asks me how my semester is going. Some people actually talk to the model, transformed by the robe into a person like the rest of us; she's tired—she's been modeling all day.

I am reminded of nothing so much as that awkward moment in a Protestant church service when the minister, having urged us from *The Book of Common Prayer* to confess our sins before Almighty God, clears his throat and asks for announcements. I grew up attending church, my first aesthetic experience. The litanies and formalized movements enthralled me. In many ways the drawing circle returns me to that rapturous hour. We are all gathered here—young and old, employed and unemployed—in joined worship of the human form. We are all, in our separate ways, trying to make a connection between mortal and immortal. We are all brought up short, as our hands move across our pages, by the fragility of the human condition. Most of all, for me, our communion takes place chiefly in silence, just as that earlier communion took place in chant. I used to be appalled when the robed minister broke character to advertise the bake sale or to instruct us to greet one another and make small talk for a moment before returning to the task of confronting our Maker.

In the drawing circle, as most chat freely during the break, there remain a few—and I find myself increasingly among them—who sit rather dumbly on our folding chairs, our eyes fixed on the middle distance. As the model disrobes and returns to her place on the elevated platform, we rise, pick up our tools, and set to our task.

My appetite for the long pose has increased considerably since the morning when I gave up on a leg at forty-five minutes. Now, in the circle, long poses generally last two hours, with perhaps three breaks, and at each stage I find myself moving deeper into what I call my drawing mind. Every thought, every movement focuses on one thing: rendering this body, held as it is in this moment of time, onto this sheet of paper. Draw what you see, I tell myself. Not what I think I should see, not the long arm stretching up and back from the shoulder, but what I *see*: a compressed cylinder for the upper arm, a triangle for the lower. Gradually—as the minutes tick by, as someone changes the playlist, as someone else stokes the stove—thoughts like "How can I get the shadow of that underarm?" or "The sag in that hip breaks my heart—should I try the extra-soft vine for it?" melt away. In their place come thoughts that I cannot express in this essay, because they are thoughts in line, in gesture. They are thoughts that lie, like bumps and potholes and smooth places, along the road that travels from this three-dimensional naked body before me, containing its history and its mortality, through my eyes and out to my arms and hand, to the shape that grows from the tool I hold in my fingers—a shape that, whatever its flatness, I believe to be as round and solid as the body at the other end of the road.

In church, nonbeliever that I was, I used to find my thoughts floating back through my week and ahead to plans and anxieties that crowded out the minister's words. Here, the language of drawing crowds out my own words. "Like Buddhist meditation," my friends suggest when I try to explain the feeling. But I am not emptying my mind; I am filling it with what feels like an antidote to a life of words, a necessary corrective. A life of silence, of materials, of the body. By the time the model takes her last break, I often realize that I have not had a verbal thought in half an hour. Driving home, as I exit the expressway through an underpass, I read the shadows cast on the pavement by tall streetlamps as swaths of soft charcoal, the world as a composition.

Hence the escape. Now to the return. A few weeks ago, in place of one of the regular models, a member of the figure drawing circle who, as it turns out, takes care of hiring the models, posed for us. That night's model had called in sick, and Karen, who's done modeling in the past, was subbing. She did an excellent job, using a minimal set of props—a long scarf, a walking stick—to strike dramatic poses, and the lights cast terrific geometric shadows across her muscular body. She also talked. Not moving her head a centimeter, she cracked jokes with a couple of the guys in the circle, promised them newer models for next spring, complained about her children. Down the center of her abdomen ran a delicate scar. At one point she commented on something's having happened "before the cancer." Dave said,

"How's that going, Karen?"

"What, you mean the cancer?"

"No, I mean your parenting. Of course I mean the cancer."

"Fine," she said. "I mean, I'm fine. It's in remission. I work out a lot."

My hand wavered over my sketch pad. I didn't want to hear this conversation. I didn't want to know Karen's story—her kids, the cancer. I didn't want to think what that scar meant. Yet here she was, before me, Karen in her body. Each body has a story. Now I was drawing a mother; I was drawing a cancer survivor.

Draw what you see.

Can sight be innocent? Should it be innocent? I sketched in the scar. I sketched Karen's chin, unusually square for a narrow jawline. I shaded the deltoids as they ran down to the biceps. During the break, Marc stepped over to look at my work. Marc teaches middle-school art and knows what he's doing, though he is always critical of his own work, and he was one of the first members of the circle who was willing to pause in front of my efforts, who could find something nice to say. Now he nodded. "You're getting somewhere," he said. "Much better shading, through the torso."

"I've been working on the boobs," I said.

"Good boobs." He nodded again. "Need to strengthen this arm, though."

"I'm afraid of the hand."

"Block it out." He gestured with his index finger. Then he glanced at Karen, in her cotton robe. "She's in great shape," he said.

"I'll say," I said.

T.S. Eliot—who seems never to have drawn a picture of any sort—famously wrote:

> The only way of expressing emotion in the form of art is by finding an "objective correlative"; in other words, a set of objects, a situation, a chain of events which shall be the formula of that particular emotion; such that when the external facts, which must terminate in sensory experience, are given, the emotion is immediately evoked.

The realistic drawing, from life, of a human being is surely the most fundamental sort of "external fact" a human hand can create; it demonstrates, as Eliot would say, "the complete adequacy of the external to the emotion." Karen's arm—if I can strengthen the arm—will completely evoke the emotion of Karen's gesture, suspended as it is in this space. By contrast, a short story, laced with subjectivities and disguises, would seem the least obvious candidate for the objective correlative. Yet what strikes me as I walk by my fellow sketchers' efforts is how replete each is with the ineffable subjectivity of its creator—not only in time and space (one sketcher views the buttocks, another the breasts), but also in feeling.

For the most part, empathy is the foremost emotion brought to the sketch. As Bill the printer said one evening, "In figure drawing, a three-hundred-pound woman with a wart on her nose is beautiful. In no other art is this true. Take a photo of her, she's hideous. Sculpture's probably disturbing. But I sketch her in charcoal, and she's beautiful." Such empathy seems to come from the long minutes spent in the shared space of the barn. The more we work on a wrinkle, a birthmark, a roll of fat, the more we embrace it, each in our own way.

That our embrace involves some form of desire is not incidental to this process. The body is our communion; our rendering it on paper is a sort of possession. But on rare occasions, perambulating the room, I spot a drawing that in its exaggerated details betrays the artist's lust and little more. Invariably these renderings, well executed though they may be, provoke no correlated desire in those of us who look. We tend, rather, to turn our heads, our empathy limited to the artist's need or shame.

Here, we find the same truth I try to teach students writing fiction: You cannot get to the heart of your subject if you focus on self-expression. By contrast, the more you apprehend your subject with your full being, the more it will yield a subject even greater than itself. And in the end, your own feelings will have been expressed—but in the most literal way, in that they are pressed out of you, insisted on by the process of putting the living, breathing thing onto the page.

Other writers who have taken up art have gone in

   Meditations for a New Century

directions very different from mine. Sherwood Anderson painted landscapes. For Robert Duncan, the "visual elements" of his more abstract art—"light and dark, opacity and translucence, color and mass" delineated "the syntax of a world and the lexicon of its things and beings." Nabokov, naturally, drew butterflies. Maxine Hong Kingston keeps sketchbooks of her dreams. What I bring to my writing from my amateur experiments in figure drawing is narrower. Focused on the naked human form, I am slowly finding my way to new ways of figuring my characters. Is not the naked body the ultimate "show, don't tell"?

Karen's cancer and its remission, for instance, resided in her scar and in the taut muscles of her thighs and upper arms. It resided, too, in the slightly aggressive stance of her feet and hips, in the strained cords of her neck. That night, I didn't want to hear Karen telling Dave about her cancer; I wanted only to draw what I saw, to produce an image on the page so evocative of what I was seeing that all who focused on the image would see the woman. And yet it was in holding the verbal knowledge of Karen's cancer in balance with the knowledge processed through the non-verbal channels of eye, hand, and charcoal that I could begin wrestling with the question of portraying a cancer survivor, of portraying this particular cancer survivor.

What I am proposing is, of course, a question of faith. On the wall of my study hangs a charcoal by Lawrence Ferlinghetti, who also drew frequently from life. In it, a nude woman reclines, resting on her wrists, her face turned away from the viewer, one leg tucked under the other. Superimposed onto the calf of the outstretched leg is the face of a young man, his eyes shut as if sleeping. I am convinced—though some have claimed the reverse—that he is dreaming of her, and that she does not know of his dream. In the sketch, in other words, I see a story. Whether Ferlinghetti intended this story, or whether it traveled along the conduit (from reclining model to arm to charcoal to sketch paper) is none of my business. Perhaps it will be the business of those who write Ferlinghetti's biography. But I want to believe that so long as I draw what I see—so long as I keep the emotion centered in the object and the act—my underlying knowledge of Karen's cancer will come to enrich and not distract from the drawing at hand. I also believe that if and when a tough mouthy cancer survivor named Karen—or Luanne, or Maria—appears in one of my stories, the exact tilt of her hip, the sculpted valley from that hip down to the wispy hair fronting her Mound of Venus, will be present in that character, whether or not I describe her in the nude.

I will never reach the artistic level of Ferlinghetti—nor even of Flannery O'Connor, who at least was art editor of her college newspaper and who commented, in "The Nature and Aim of Fiction," that "any discipline can help your writing . . . particularly drawing . . . It forces [you] to look at things." I have considered the notion of taking a class in drawing. Thus far I've rejected it, not because I cling to my amateurishness—on the contrary, my sketches often mortify me—but because the teaching would necessarily include words. Right now, in their slow, blunt way, the models are teaching me. The materials are teaching me. The work of my Thursday-night companions, as I wander the room during the break, is teaching me. I liken this sort of learning to a language immersion program, where nothing ever gets translated for the learner. The task of translation, if there is to be such, will be mine.

Bit by bit, my drawing has improved. A foot now lies within the realm of possibility. At the end of the evening I pack up my sketchbooks and charcoals. I bid my fellow worshippers at the altar of figure drawing good night. I drive home, moving from a language that sees the world in shapes and densities, light and shadow, to one comprising snatches of conversation, arguments, explanations, figures (as we say) of speech. I show my partner my sketch of the long pose and hold my breath that he might see through it to what I have been seeing. When I turn, next day, to my work with words, bodies surround me—naked, breathing, mortal, and alive.

Meditation on Gandara

The bas-relief rests against the upper panel of my piano. With its uneven base, it cannot balance upright. It's carved from shale, gray and rough, the back chipped at the corners, revealing the layers by which, in slow-moving water and across millennia, mud and quartz compacted into rock. Dirt lodges in the crevices around the carved figures, in the bend of their tiny arms and the sweep of their tiny garments. The figures—we'll call them bodhisattvas—are three. On left and right, the carver fashioned them with similar robes but different headdresses and discernibly different features. Each carries something in his right arm that has long since chipped off, leaving the arm amputated just below the crooked elbow. A frieze of lotus petals fronts the platform on which they stand alert and watchful. The central figure—call him Buddha—sits in lotus position atop a tiered seat, the tiers marked by two layers of striated petals. His hands meet at his chest in Vajra mudra, the gesture of knowledge, with the left forefinger and thumb forming a circle and the right hand pressed against the heart. All three bodhisattvas are backed by flat halos. The Buddha appears in a state of bliss. The whole artifact measures about the size of a small postcard. Its thickest point falls just shy of an inch. It sits heavy in the palm, the weight of a dictionary.

I received this artifact on my penultimate day in Pakistan, in spring 2012. I spent the day with Mr. Aslam Khan, a gentleman of Peshawar, in the Khyber-Pakhtunkhwa District adjacent to the Khyber Pass and the notorious tribal areas of Pakistan. I had come to Pakistan to do research on the honor culture of the Pashtuns, a tribe centered in Khyber-Pakhtunkhwa and southwestern Afghanistan. Extremist Pashtuns form the core of the Taliban. Mr. Aslam (the address became comfortable after he began addressing me as Mrs. Lucy) had been the landlord of a journalist I know who spent time in Pakistan in the late twentieth century. Though he had not hosted my stay in Peshawar—I stayed with a university professor and her family—he was eager to do me service. Already he had given a dinner in my honor at his brother's restaurant, where a private room was reserved for a party of perhaps thirty people, mostly his and my host's extended families. Before the dinner began, he had presented me with three books on Pashtun culture that I had been unable to find in the West. During dinner I had been seated among the women, most of whom spoke very little English and whose questions centered entirely on what children I had, what professions they were entering, and where we lived. My answers to these questions were wildly unsatisfactory: my two grown sons were scraping together livings as a tennis instructor and an actor; neither lived with me; in fact, no one lived with me except my husband (to whom, I neglected to say, I was not actually married). But servants came around with perhaps a dozen dishes, all of which I had to try. The day after the dinner, a courier arrived at my host's house with another gift from Mr. Aslam, a large wool rug of high quality with an intricate design of deep purples, reds, greens, and golds, which I would have to somehow transport through Europe and back to America.

And yet, plainly, Mr. Aslam felt he had not done enough to demonstrate the honor my visit conveyed to him. When I mentioned that I regretted having been unable to visit Pakistan's one World Heritage site, the ruins and museum at Taxila, he announced that he would pick me up with his driver and we would spend the day there. So here he arrives, early in the morning, with another gift, a pair of traditional Pashtun men's sandals for one of my sons. His driver is indeed with him, but for the two-hour drive to the site, Mr. Aslam stays at the wheel, with me in the passenger seat and the driver in the back. Mr. Aslam is short and extremely portly, giving him a Humpty Dumpty look in his off-white kurta. His trim white beard and mustache contrast his nut-brown skin, darker than most Pashtuns, and the coffee streaks of eyebrow and balding hair. As with many of his body type, I find it difficult to guess his age.

He is eager, as we drive toward Islamabad, to discuss culture, particularly religion. He is very devout, curious about my religious views. He considers Muslims, Jews, and Christians all as People of the Book, alike in more ways than we differ—unlike, say, the Hindus, whom he considers to be pagans lacking religious law. For this reason, he believes marriage across the Abrahamic faiths should be not only

   Meditations for a New Century

allowed but encouraged. He has firm ideas, too, about issues like gay marriage and no-fault divorce. The *Quran*, he points out, condemns neither of these. Pakistan needs to advance.

In one sense, this conversation resembles many that I've had during my three-week stay in Pakistan. My hosts and their acquaintances wax urgent on these subjects. Apart from the question of drone strikes, about which they would like me please to do something, questions of religious culture are central to their concerns; to possess no religious feeling is incomprehensible. In another sense, the dialogue with Mr. Aslam differs because the long drive is uninterrupted, and he seems less self-consciously Pashtun than others. He's keenly interested in personal responsibility. He allows there are times he wishes himself free of responsibility for his three grown sons, including one who is married. And yet he fully expects them to care for him when he gets old; that's part of the bargain. As he describes his life, the burden of family seems to weigh on his sloped forehead and soft shoulders. It is family, I think, that has made him so heavy, family he carries with him like a stone. For us in the West, I admit when he asks, there are times of relative freedom from responsibility for other family members—in our twenties, for instance, and perhaps again in our fifties, when our children are grown and our parents have passed away. But just as these times do not exist for him, so too does their isolation not exist. We watch the mountains rise up and fall away as we mull over this truth. Gradually, Mr. Aslam raises the question of life after death. It is, he says, extremely important to him. It is why he puts up with all this headache. There must be such life, for how else can there be punishment or reward for the ways in which one has conducted one's life on earth? Do I not think so?

I think, I tell him, that we receive our punishments and our rewards in this life. Not necessarily in riches and comfort or poverty and pain, but in pangs of remorse or the free sentiment of an easy conscience. He glances sideways at me. I sound, even to myself, tremendously naïve. And for a moment, the history of this place—of Pakistan, of its fierce tribes, its bloody wars and oppressions at the hands of everyone from the British to the Taliban fanatics, its earthquakes and floods and droughts, its haughty warlords and scrabbling beggars—rides in the car with us, defying my simple logic.

And then we are at Taxila. Still a town of stonecutters, Mr. Aslam explains as we round the switchback to the village, perched at the edge of a high plateau outside Islamabad. We thread through the market center, the goats and chickens and skinny boys, and on to the museum and the sacred sites.

How to bring you to this place? By the lights of affluent, well-traveled Americans, we have here another museum of ancient history—organized by era and location, carefully signed, the display cases rubbed spotless and brochures available in Urdu, Hindi, Pashto, Chinese, English. Your children would yawn. Your father, if he is like mine, would insist on stopping at every exhibit, however repetitive or inconsequential. You have been, no doubt, to too many of these clean, well-lit places.

But I have been in Lahore and Peshawar, where load shedding shuts down electricity half the day, where the museums are dark and moldy and inhabited only by ghosts, where once-genteel balconies sag and splinter under the weight of laundry and crisscrossed power lines, where the hot air mixes dust and diesel, where eight-year-old children wear the faces of old men. To come upon this broad avenue lined with bougainvillea and neatly trimmed hedges, to enter this air-conditioned hall, is to board a spaceship set incongruously down on a dry plain. I feel something akin to panic.

As the exhibits themselves explain, Taxila is among the earliest sites of Buddhist civilization, dating back to the Gandara period, first century A.D. Its images of the Buddha are more Greek than Indian, with some Alexander the Great influence thrown in. The statues in the museum depict a young, muscular man in elegantly draped robes over six-pack abs, mustachioed, a peaceful face above military shoulders. Smaller cases hold jewels, tools, and toys excavated from the nearby sites. Mr. Aslam exhorts me to take pictures of all the exhibits, even though he has bought me a slick oversized catalog of the museum as yet another gift. Halfway through our tour we are greeted by the museum director, an acquaintance of Mr. Aslam, who insists we join him for tea before we move on.

It's remarkable, this story of the Buddha's origins here in the mountains of Pakistan, long before the Indians or the Chinese got hold of him. At the same time, I'm keenly aware that the visit is going well, according to Mr. Aslam's plan: His prestigious friend has made a proper fuss, and the exemplary character of the museum itself has

---

    Meditations for a New Century

shown this American guest that Pakistan can hold its head up among the cultures of the world if only it's given the means to do so. Mr. Aslam's relief is palpable. Even his brow unknits.

We drive on, to the archaeological site. Three major excavated cities spread over thousands of acres, but Mr. Aslam is not an athletic man, and the heat of the day is rising. One young man with a badge lackadaisically guards the closest site, while another proposes himself as a tour guide. Mr. Aslam quickly negotiates a price. We view the foundations of ordinary houses, the stairs running down to what were sunken baths, the worn and pitted figures guarding a temple, the sun dials and irrigation ditches, the globular stupas, the narrow avenues down which these ancient people drove their goats and hauled their grains. In one corner of the site, archaeologists have dug deeper, and we can detect another layer below the surface foundations . . . and a layer below that . . . and below that, the ghost of another layer. In other words, there are perhaps ten thousand years of civilizations prior to the Gandara whose ruins remain buried on this plateau. To dig for the earlier remains would mean destroying the remains we have, and so for the most part archaeologists let them lie. Who quarried these earliest stones, we can only guess. And it strikes me as we turn to leave the site that today there are almost no Buddhists in Pakistan, that we have been visiting a past split off, culturally and philosophically, from the people who harbor its remains.

At the edge of the site, three boys materialize out of what seems nowhere. The objects they bear in their arms—a stone head, chipped jewels, carved stone bowls—vaguely resemble the artifacts of the museum. Rapidly they engage Mr. Aslam in Urdu. He explains to me that these boys are selling what are surely false relics. I should remember, he says, that the people here are excellent stonecutters. But do I want a souvenir, anyway?

I have been deluged with gifts, these weeks. Already I have had to buy a duffel to cart them home, and I still don't know how I'll manage Mr. Aslam's rug. I don't know the protocol for responding to this offer, whether a polite refusal is expected or would be resented. The soft brown eyes of the boys swing from Mr. Aslam to me and back again. A small souvenir would be very nice, I say, but only if it's quite small and will not cost much. In other words, no life-sized Buddha heads.

Mr. Aslam negotiates with the boys in Urdu and passes them

   Meditations for a New Century

what looks like 5,000 rupees, about $40, more than he should spend. And the stone with its three figures is placed in my palm. "It's extraordinary," I say.

"It is a fake," Mr. Aslam says, wiping sweat from his brow. "But you will remember Taxila."

The stone frieze is not the last of Mr. Aslam's gifts. At 2:30 the following morning, the mention of his nephew, who has a high-level position at the Peshawar airport, gets us through the first set of security gates at the airport for my 4 a.m. flight. Sohrab, my professor-friend's grown son, is seeing me off, and he parks the car in a special lot, from which I can enter directly into the terminal's internal security clearance. Sohrab lingers at the door of what resembles a cavernous, tunneled basement while I answer questions about my visit and the goods I am carrying out of Pakistan. "You are alone?" the man on the other side of a long table wishes to know.

"No," I say, and point to Sohrab in the doorway. "But I am taking the plane alone."

He grins sardonically. Then, leaving my new rug in its tight roll, he begins unpacking my small suitcase and large duffel. Out come two smaller rugs, two hand-embroidered pillows, several shawls, baskets, handmade shoes, jewelry. Finally he arrives at the little stone frieze. He holds it up to the light of a swinging overhead lamp. "Where," he asks, "did you obtain this?"

"At Taxila," I say. Only then does alarm sound through my veins. "It's a fake," I add. "Boys were selling it. Stonecutters."

"You paid how much for this?"

"I don't know. My friend bought it for me."

He glances at Sohrab in the doorway.

"Not him. Mr. Aslam Khan bought it. I told him not to spend any money. Just for a souvenir."

The official leaves with my rock. I look back at Sohrab, who shrugs. Suddenly, I know. The frieze is not a fake. That dirt in the crevices, the broken arms, the cut of the stone robes, the tiny faces— these were not carved by those boys nor by their fathers. That dirt has packed its way into the stone over two thousand years. The boys came from the site, not from the road. With only one guard for a thousand acres, how could anyone stop a group of enterprising kids from digging into the dirt, from chiseling away what they could and

 Meditations for a New Century

washing away whatever would quit the stone?

I know, too, that I'm not giving up my bodhisattvas, not without a fight. The oily-haired official will only sell the relic on the black market. It will never return to the clean, bright museum at Taxila, never take its place in the pristine display case.

Two officials return. They ask again where I got this thing, what was paid for it, how I know it to be a fake. Aslam Khan, I say again, assured me. Aslam Khan paid a little for it, a token sum. A souvenir.

There are people behind me now, workers from the tribal areas flying to the Emirates to labor for a few months. They are shuffling their feet, grumbling. The officials glare at me, then toss the frieze into the duffel. Quickly I tuck in the shawls, the other gifts. I wave to Sohrab. I obey the official's order to "Get in woman line."

Now the frieze sits on my piano, my three bodhisattvas looking placidly out on these bizarre surroundings—my rocking chair, picture window, polished wood floor, the electric lights. Only Mr. Aslam's rug in the next room reminds them of home. I've considered donating the artifact to a museum here but I fear it would appear tainted, goods stolen from a sacred site. Made to give up my stone spirits, I have no faith that they would find their way back to a land from which their influence has long since taken flight.

Since arriving here they have grown in power. What appeared to me, at Taxila, as the remnant of a lost civilization has come to life. The delicate etching of the necklaces about the two standing figures' necks. The particular coil of one headdress, the carefully delineated toes of the bare feet, the miniature earrings and graceful neck of the central Buddha, meditating on knowledge. What instrument carved you, my little deities? What hand on the instrument, what vision in the eyes of the carver? I think of Mr. Aslam's certainty of life after death, and seem to find it carved in stone. We are People of the Book, perhaps, but we are also People of Time, and it is across time that we touch most profoundly.

Sometimes I think of taking a toothbrush to my ancient frieze, or a bit of steel wool, to scrub away the last of the dirt and expose more of the delicate carving. But even the dirt, it seems to me now, has power. It calls me thief, it calls me caretaker. It calls me mortal, and reminds me whereto I shall return.

 Meditations for a New Century

Meditation on Hair

In the novel *Innocent*, Scott Turow's best-selling sequel to his debut, *Presumed Innocent*, the protagonist, Rusty Sabich, just turned sixty, is having an affair with a young lawyer who has clerked for him. "Physically," he describes her, "she is glorious, a power Anna enjoys and works hard to hold on to—manicures and pedicures, hair appointments, facials, 'routine maintenance,' as she calls it. Her breasts are perfect, large, beautifully belled, with a broad, dark aureole and long nipples. And I am fascinated by her female parts, where her youth somehow seems centered. She's waxed there, 'a full Brazilian,' is her term. It's a first for me, and the smooth feel provokes my lust like a lightning bolt."

A "full Brazilian" isn't just Anna's term. As most women know, it's the latest fashion in depilation, the removal by wax of all the hair around one's genital areas, in a procedure that causes intense pain and can lead to staph infections. According to one legend of the term's origin, sixteenth century Portuguese explorers in Brazil discovered females whose genitalia "were so exposed, so healthy and so *hairless*, that looking upon them we felt no shame."

Why didn't the explorers feel shame? I have been thinking about this subject in more than a casually political way since a close friend and his twenty-month-old daughter, Cissy, spent a long weekend with my partner and me. I reared two sons; my image of a baby includes a little rubbery penis that arcs pee onto the far wall while you're trying to diaper. Cissy is not quite two. Her Mound of Venus and the crevice that passes from it through her legs form a lovely creased pillow that I was able to contemplate in a way that had heretofore eluded me. My looking on it, my partner's looking on it, evoked no shame: We were looking at a baby. Our feelings were of nurture and not of desire.

And that's what a full Brazilian aims at—a look, and a feel,

                    Meditations for a New Century

reminiscent of a girl baby. You can't recapture that precious plumpness, and the soft structures tucked inside the cleft have grown complicated. But insofar as the heterosexual gaze involves lust—and insofar as that lust, experienced outside whatever norms you accept, provokes shame—it's reasonable to assert that a male gaze devoid of shame is a male gaze devoid of lust. It would be gross naiveté to impute purity to the Portuguese who raped and pillaged their way through South America. Moreover, it's possible that calling a certain wax job "Brazilian" has given it an edge of so-called spiciness that reeks of European attitudes toward dark exoticism. But the original pronouncement still carries weight: These were Catholic men, reared in a culture where shame meant something, describing the sight of women who were hairless below the navel, and that hairlessness momentarily arrested shameful impulses. They felt, or claimed to feel, the way my partner and our young friend feel when they are looking at Cissy.

But what about Rusty Sabich? Let's go back to Anna and those "female parts" on which her youth "somehow seems centered." I'd venture that the mysterious "somehow" question is answered by the next couple of lines. The very hairlessness, the little-girlishness of Anna's *mons veneris* is what turns Rusty on. Rusty feels no shame at being hit by a "lightning bolt" of lust on viewing Anna's depilated genitalia because he is without a sense of shame. His shamelessness, in fact, is part of the point—he may have reached three score years, but he still gets off on breaking a taboo.

That taboo, of course, is being broken at this very moment in thousands of bedrooms across America. Or is it a taboo? Other cultures not only condone sex between adult men and young girls (menarche sometimes being a token requirement), but frame depilation as a religious act of cleansing. In Islam, the practice of *fitrah* includes removing underarm and pubic hair; plenty of women's bodies hidden under burqas have undergone extreme waxing. In the West, fashion inflicts risk and pain in any number of ways, from breast augmentation to four-inch heels. Look at Anna's other choices—the mani-pedi, the hair styling. I'm not getting exercised over those. Men are waxing their chests these days. Maybe it's just a trend.

And yet. In Turow's novel, Anna herself gets some of the narration. Not once does she mention her concern over personal care. Never does she weigh in on why she undergoes genital waxing, whether it delights her sexually or whether she does it only to please a man like Rusty. She seems neither insecure about her sexuality nor eager to project a fashionable look or feel when unclothed. Her only remark on body hair comes from her observation of another lover-in-waiting, who has "a cute little flavor saver under his lip." I had to look that one up at urbandictionary.com, which explains that a flavor saver is a patch of hair under the lips that "allows one to relive eating a chick's pussy by 'saving the flavor' in the hair." Now, I am not certain that a woman would refer to a bit of facial hair that way, but since a Brazilian wax leaves the depilated skin extraordinarily tender, facial hair on the man performing cunnilingus can, by most accounts, be quite irritating for the woman.

In other words, the full Brazilian is not a physical or character attribute that truly belongs to Anna. It exists in the novel because it titillates Rusty, and Rusty's vigorous desires are meant to accord with the reader's own. As a female reader, I'm accustomed to reading like a man. Imaginatively, I can empathize with Rusty's loving Anna's large "belled" breasts, just as I can get behind another protagonist's fondness for his lover's petite uplifted nipples. Interesting either way. But placing myself in Rusty's sensibility while the full Brazilian gives him a swift hard-on—especially when no rationale for the Brazilian exists outside Rusty's fantasy life—horrifies me. I want to keep baby Cissy (and ten-year-old Cissy, and teenaged Cissy) away from the eyes of such a man.

Pubic hair was my first sign of puberty. Other girls' breasts grew large first; still others got their periods before their body hair kicked in. But for me it was the pubes—dark, curly, lush even, while my chest was still flat and my hips still narrow. "Oh my," my mother said when I showed her the little triangle that had sprung up, it seemed, overnight. "You'll have to wash more, down there." I had never seen my mother's own pubic hair, though I had caught glimpses of the large, sagging women who actually showered nude in the ladies' locker room at the public swimming pool; I had seen how the soap foamed up in the hair "down there," and it frightened me.

As I moved through adolescence, the hair on my body generally thickened and coarsened, even as the hair on my head thinned. I was a WASP, Twiggy-thin (thus, no doubt, the loss of hair from my scalp), with none of the heavy body-hair genes I associated with Mediterranean ancestry. Every strand of it embarrassed me. To make things worse, my sister and I were allowed to shave only to the point where our miniskirts fell. We called it the timber line. In my summer bikini, I looked down to see curly hair peek beneath the leg band and thick leg hair trail down the insides of my thighs.

In fact—I see now, looking over old photos from one summer after the next, the gawky bikini-clad girl grinning at the camera—the hair must have been hardly noticeable, because it is imperceptible in the snapshots. But at the time, my gross sexuality mortified me. As soon as I left home for college and could shave all the way up my legs and into the inner crease where thigh joined torso, I felt a burst of confidence. Had someone offered to relieve me of the bush of hair that had marked me for almost eight years, I would have suffered whatever pain was required.

No one offered. Enter the feminist awakening of the 1970s, when women were encouraged to let all their hair grow—on their heads, under their arms, on their legs, and naturally on their "female parts." My first boyfriend at college urged me to join this hirsute movement, only to back away when my legs became, as he put it, furry. His recoiling was, I suspect, part and parcel of the general aversion hippies were challenging—the notion, that is, that body hair (male or female) makes us more like other animals. In James Dickey's *Deliverance*, which came out in 1970, Ed, the hirsute protagonist, is repeatedly called an "ape," and the metaphysical tension between human reason and nature's violence forms the heart of the book. That glabrousness is next to cleanliness and hence to godliness is not a new concept, nor is it necessarily sexist. Yet the position of earth-woman feminists and their supporters ran up not just against ideas of tidiness or human exceptionality but against heterosexual male resistance. So long as men could not bring themselves to desire "natural" women, the sexual liberation espoused by the movement was doomed to founder.

Perhaps not completely coincidentally, the object of Ed's desire in *Deliverance* is the nubile model for Kitt'n Britches, "healthy and a little tomboyish," whose "bare back had a helpless, undeveloped look about it, and this seemed to me more womanly and endearing than anything else about her." Roman Polanski's arrest for the rape of a thirteen-year-old girl took place in 1977 amid widespread acceptance of the ripe sexuality of underage girls. We had the Pill; we rejected marriage; we wanted to get laid while we were young. Thus, many women who wanted sex doubled down on the usual expectations of looking young. More to the point of pubic waxing, "getting laid" meant getting pleasure from a man, not just providing it. *The Joy of Sex* celebrated cunnilingus (with illustrations including pubic hair); Masters & Johnson suggested that it should be the major element in sexual activities involving women.

And this activity alarmed men. There we were—and are—to contend with: the two sets of genital lips, the rim around the vagina, the sneaky little clitoris, and the smell—my god, the smell. Captured in the pubic hair. Made more frightening by the prospect of getting a pubic strand in the mouth or caught in the throat. Consider the expressions used for performing oral sex on a woman: muff diving, drinking from the furry cup, tipping the velvet, carpet munching. In *The Sopranos*, syndicate heavyweight Uncle Junior finds himself labeled a carpet muncher after it's learned that he has performed cunnilingus on his post-menopausal girlfriend. His response is to have the woman's face sprayed with acid. Message? Macho men don't munch carpet. They don't go down.

But we want them to go down. Asking for and expecting oral sex is a statement of feminist sexuality. Google "full Brazilian" or investigate any of the websites devoted to the glorious experience of waxing oneself bare, and you will find plenty of language devoted to the relief men experience on finding the waxed woman so "clean," so "inviting." Quote after quote testifies to a boyfriend's request that the woman have the procedure, and to the consequent sexual pleasure the woman experiences. The chthonic depths of women's sexual parts are initially frightening—ask any adolescent boy, if you can get one to talk—and hence disgusting. Anything we can do to ease the transition from men's taking pleasure to their giving it, we want to do.

Meanwhile, adolescent girls are experiencing, at an increasingly young age, the equally frightening (and potentially disgusting) terrain of male orgasm and ejaculation into their mouths. But sex studies have shown, for reasons that researchers debate, that girls tend to achieve—and to seek—orgasm later than boys. And those girls would be asking the boys not simply to take their genitals into the mouth, but to explore, to discover, to be proactive in the love making. For me, it was astonishing that a fleeting boyfriend just after college would lift my hips toward him and put his mouth on me—and one aspect of the astonishment was his ability to negotiate the hair. One might even conjecture—mightn't one?—that the experience of "Chad," quoted in *Salon* as saying of his girlfriend's Brazilian, "It was like, oh my God, an unbelievably primal welling of emotion . . . the whole little girl eroticism of it," is not really pedophilic. It's just suggestive of his desire to experience her orally as he was first experienced, as a young, fresh lover.

No. Against that phrase "little girl eroticism," the conjecture doesn't work. It tries to excuse a phenomenon that cannot, really, be excused.

Did I mention pain? For those not in the know, a few details: The full Brazilian uses a combination of hot beeswax and liquid rosin to strip every bit of hair from the buttocks and adjacent to the anus, perineum and vulva (labia majora and mons pubis). Folliculitis, a staph infection of the hair follicles, is one risk of the procedure, and can require incision and drainage. After a searing hour in which hair is ripped out of the most sensitive membranes of their bodies, most women experience lingering discomfort for five days or less. But the procedure needs to be repeated, for maximal benefit, three weeks later.

Advertisements for full Brazilians claim that pubic hair is "completely unnecessary." This argument, of course, has won the day with leg and underarm hair. Maybe there was a time we needed the hair on the legs for warmth, but now we have pants; maybe we needed the stuff under the arms to catch pheromones, but now we have White Musk by Coty. The advice columnist for the hip publication *CosmoGirl*, however, puts the lie to the advertisers' claim:

> You should know that pubic hair is there for a few good health reasons. It provides a cushion that helps prevent your labia (the fleshy skin or "lips" around your vagina) from getting chafed, which can happen when you wear tight clothes or ride a bike. The hairs also act sort of like a spider web, trapping harmful bacteria so they can't get into your vagina and cause infections like vaginosis. Plus, urinary tract infections are often caused by bacteria from the anus—and if you have no pubes, there's a clear pathway for that bacteria to travel to your urethra (where you urinate from) and infect it.

In other words, far from being "cleaner," a full Brazilian is apt to spread the dirty stuff around.

But clean, too, can be a metaphor—for virginal, untouched, not fouled by all those excretions that embarrassed us as we progressed through adolescence. *Our Bodies, Ourselves*, among other publications, links full waxing to the boom in vaginal and labial surgery. You can tighten the vagina, reinstall the hymen, plump the labia—all, surely, not in search of a fresh blush of youth for the world to see, nor for your own pleasure, but for your man's experience of you. So now an act tied to cunnilingus—a pleasure for which feminists practically lobbied a generation ago—has to do with sex as female performance rather than female pleasure.

Ironically, the literal performance of sex, in the movies, has begun to require pubic hair, for two reasons. One is that MPAA ratings consider hair covering the genitalia to be equivalent to clothing, so that a flash of an unwaxed nude woman below the waist can nab the film a less restrictive rating than the same flash with the flesh exposed. Another is authenticity: Filmmakers recognize that a full frontal shot of a woman in a film set, say, during the 1960s would not feature a full Brazilian. Since Kate Winslet, for instance, who starred in *The Reader*, had a "landing strip" (a tiny line of hair running vertically while the rest is waxed—and how is it that Kate Winslet's wax job is public knowledge?), she wore a merkin for the movie. A merkin, for those out of touch with medieval fashions, is a pubic wig, once popular among prostitutes who had shaved their pubic hair to discourage lice but who needed to look sexy (and occasionally to hide signs of syphilis).

A full wax is now *de rigueur* for prostitutes and porn stars—whether because of MPAA ratings or "little girl eroticism" is anyone's guess. If viewers (unlike, presumably, Rusty Sabich) are "shamed" at all by their gaze in the twenty-first century—that is, if the exposure of a sexually desirable woman arouses the gazer's unsanctioned lust—they are *more* shamed by glabrous genitalia than by the hirsute mons. We are the Portuguese explorers' opposites—or at least the opposite of the figures they drew of themselves. Hairless adult women reminded those shame-inclined figures of children, whereas women with pubic hair (like prostitutes) turned them on. Hairless adult women put us in mind of YouPorn, whereas women with pubic hair get an R rating at worst.

Another movie reference. In Billy Bob Thornton's *Slingblade* (1996), the symbolically named character Charles Bushman recounts:

She had on a leather skirt and had a lot of hair on her arms. I

 Meditations for a New Century

like that a lot. That means a big bush. I like a big bush. She says, "Are you dating?" you know, so I said, "Sure." She gets in and we pull off to a remote location that was comfortable for both she and I. She says, "How much do you wanna spend?" I said, "Whatever it will take to see that bush of yours because I know it's a big one." She says, "$25." That's not chicken feed to a working man so I produce the $25, she puts it in her shoe, pulls up her skirt and there before me lay this thin, crooked, uncircumcised penis.

Bushman murders the man, but the point here is more subtle. He's a pervert—and we know he's a pervert even before he murders, because he's attracted to a "woman" with plentiful body hair. It would be nice to think that the attraction itself is lustily heterosexual and the violent response to the transvestite homophobic. But Bushman's compulsive reiteration of the story suggests that his main horror is the way in which his desire for the "big bush" has failed to mask his desire for a man (he's angered not simply by the penis but by its being "thin" and "crooked"); and his description of the murder inscribes not only homophobia but also misogyny and self-hatred. Whatever triumphs may have lain in feminists' claim to their own body hair, or in later attempts to separate femininity from choices about depilation, Charles Bushman's initial transaction posits the hairy prostitute as a creature of uncertain sex and as a target, not of healthy lust, but of perverse and therefore dangerous desire.

Must the hirsute woman, then, remain at odds with mainstream notions of female identity? Perhaps not, in the very long run. I've passed menopause now. Along with my peers, I've noticed I don't "need" to shave my legs nearly as often as before. My arm hair has thinned to blond wisps, and I forget I have hair under my arms at all. In my latest confab about pubic hair, one friend said, "I don't know why I worry about waxing it. I'm losing it all anyway!"

In other words: *Do you want to be hairless? Try getting old.* Just as pheromone-releasing sweat decreases in our second half-century, so does the hair designed, in part, to catch hold of it. A woman with dark, luxurious pubic hair is not a little girl, but neither is she over the hill. As fashions change, maybe we'll see the return of the merkin, not for period-piece movies, but as a trick for feeling youthful. Next, extensions for your thinning bush. Rogaine for the mons. We will find new ways to inflict discomfort and pain on ourselves, to risk infection, to lay the sacrifice of the body with which we were born on the altar of loveliness. And then, like the shaved and tweezered and waxed and sculpted mortals who have gone before us, we will leave it all behind.

Meditation on a Series of Apartments

There is a balm in Gilead
To heal the sin-sick soul.

—African American spiritual

The Ones I Didn't Take

1. The *East Side Express* was vacating this place, a ground-floor studio in the East 70s. The staff needed someone willing to live with the cats they had to leave behind. Ronald Reagan was about to be elected president. New York, like me, was emerging from a bankrupt marriage. Still, young people lived in Manhattan in 1980. They wanted to be on the island so they could walk to their jobs; the subways rarely functioned. I owned a tiny cat, named Octopus. Octopi, I had learned on a whale-watching excursion once, have the same IQ as cats. I'd always wondered what test was administered. The *East Side Express* people said they would come in and feed Octopus, along with the other cats, while I was at work. Inspecting the place, I found it big, light, and clean. One entire wall was lined with cans of cat food and was abutted by three odorless litter pans. Prowling the space were nine of the largest felines I had ever laid eyes on. One by one they rubbed against my legs. They miaowed ominously. I pictured waking in the wee hours, my face covered by an enormous weight of cat, like octopus tentacles. I pictured Octopus' entrails, how tasty the others would find them.

2. A huge, high-ceilinged studio in the West 90s came with a polished baby grand piano and a set of music stands. Four days a week, while I was at work, the place would be used for lessons and rehearsals. In the evenings I could whack away at Beethoven. The day of my appointment to sign the lease, I came down with stomach flu. I lay nauseated on the pullout couch in my cousin Joan's condo in Bronxville. Joan's three

 Meditations for a New Century

daughters were away at college, and she was dating a married man. She wanted me out of her place yesterday. In the distance, somewhere in her condo complex, a child was repeating scales, making the same mistake in the key of D sharp, each time bringing her elbows onto the keyboard. I pictured myself home sick from work, lying quietly behind the Japanese screen in my gleaming West Side apartment while the teacher said patiently, "Do it again. Try it again."

3. At the end of September, I signed a lease for a so-called garden apartment on Bleecker Street. The entrance was fronted by a head shop and the Warlock Bar. The rat-faced manager and I had shaken hands with the understanding that I would move in on October first. I paid first and last months' rent with a cashier's check—most of my savings—but I had a job; I'd be good to go by November first. When I got back to Joan's I showed her the lease. "This started the first of September," she said. I called the rat-faced manager. He said he'd keep my money and evict me if I didn't pay rent for October in three days. I called the *East Side Express* and placed an ad for a sublet in the Village. Next day I showed the place to a sweet kid with floppy brown hair and Coke-bottle glasses. I needed first and last, I told him. Two hours later he was back with cash. By the time the last month came around, I figured, I'd have enough saved up that I wouldn't miss the refund. Rat Face called to tell me he'd have me and my pansy friend arrested. A few weeks later the kid broke the lease and disappeared. By then the manager had stopped calling me.

Interlude: Fall 2019

Though I live, now, a short morning's train ride from Manhattan, I elect to take over a friend's lease for a month, to settle back into the city for a while. When they learn the location, people whistle. 76th Street, between Columbus and Amsterdam. The streets and the bustle feel familiar to me, and I take petty pride in moving like a New Yorker, brisk and confident.

The apartment consists of what used to be some upper-middle-class family's small living room. A chandelier hangs from the ceiling, and a frieze of plaster cupids and garlands runs along the tops of the walls. A tiny bathroom and tinier kitchen have been shoehorned into what might have been the passageway to the rest of the apartment. Across the street, bright blue Citi Bikes fill a rack; I use my app to unlock one and take it for a spin around a traffic-free Central Park or along the bike path that Michael Bloomberg rebuilt by the Hudson River, from South Ferry to well north of the George Washington Bridge. Say what you will about Bloomberg and his billions, he made Manhattan an island of parks. With the weather still balmy in early November, I walk across Central Park after dark. Teenagers are smoking weed on the benches; a father strollers his colicky infant. The safety I feel disorients me.

The First Place I Took

I'd learned by now. Wednesday was the day the *Village Voice* listed rentals. Apartment-seekers stayed up past midnight on Tuesday to grab a copy. Next morning, they showed up wherever they needed to be in time to beat the rush. My first pick was 138 East 93rd Street, catty-corner to the 92nd Street Y, where Yehudi Menuhin gave recitals and W.S. Merwin read poetry. In front of the building, before dawn, I took second in line. First in line was a guy who'd been burned out of his apartment. A girl he'd met at a bar had spent the night with him. When the firefighters axed the door and found his collapsed body blocking it, the girl was gone. Burns mottled his back, raised and pink, like fish skin. He took the listed apartment, on the fourth floor. I got one just above. His was a small studio. Mine, same size, boasted a plaster wall down the middle. The bathroom was too small for me to stretch out my arms, even diagonally. I could cook on a hot plate. No closet. My queen mattress and box spring, all I'd salvaged from the marriage, proved too wide to make the bends in the stairs. The guy below and his dad helped me push them straight up five flights between the railings. The bed fit into one room like a deck of cards into its box. I climbed into it from the foot. That winter I hired a kid to help me knock down the wall. Plaster got into my bed, my nostrils, my hair, my eyes.

"Why the hell," I asked the super as I carried another box of the heavy plaster down and out to the trash, "did they put this wall *up*?"

"You looked out the window?" The super was a rangy guy with a gold tooth. In my apartment, he opened the rattling sash. I leaned out into sleet. All the way down the back of the building, large metal braces stuck out from the brick in a zigzag. I pulled my head back in.

"Those were for the ramp," the super said. "For the horses."

Rolling blackouts marked that winter. The news was filled with Reagan's inauguration and rumors about a hostage deal, the herpes epidemic, and a new cancer. The cancer, they said, affected gay men and Haitians. A lovely Haitian guy handled the mail room at work. I studied him, not daring to bring up the subject, praying he'd be spared. When the heat went off in my horse stalls I sought refuge in the horse stalls below, with the guy who'd survived the fire. He asked me to rub his back with prescription grease. When we made love he used a condom that failed.

A woman at work told me about an abortifacient, brewed with herbs from a Wiccan shop on West 9th, that tasted like poisoned mud. When I'd drunk it for a month with no effect, I signed on for an abortion. The cramps afterward laid me low in the horse stalls, where I picked up the rotary-dial Princess phone I'd bought on the Lower East Side, called in sick to work, sipped blackberry brandy, and wept.

"When summer comes you are gonna roast under this roof," the super said in late February. "I take care of another place. A better place."

Interlude: Fall Again, 2019

Every other storefront on the Upper West Side features self-improvement. Pure Yoga, Blue Mercury Cosmetics, Equinox Gym & Spa, SoulCycle, Juice Press, BloBlow Dry Bar, La Jolie Nails, European Wax. Along the sidewalks, improved women, leggy sylphs, walk purebred dogs. Three days a week, outdoor markets spring up by the Museum of Natural History or Lincoln Center. No urine pollutes the subway, which announces its regular departures on a blinking screen. The ample population of homeless has self-deported from this part of the island. We are in the Trump era, which looks utterly different from the Reagan era the way a moth looks utterly different from a caterpillar. Three times a week, garbage and recycle collectors whisk enormous plastic bags from the sidewalks. When I peer at these bags, they seem filled with the same debris. Cardboard hoists open the lid of the bin for glass and metals; the bin for plastic reeks of rotted food. The people who inhabit a place as clean and uplifting as this never fret, apparently, over recycling.

I wear black, don sunglasses, and whisper as I stride down the sidewalk, "I am wealthy."

The Second Place

Urine pooled on the stairs to the subway, along the tunnel from Grand Central to 45th Street, underneath the bridges in Central Park, and in the entrance to my new building at 84th and 2nd. Every morning I stepped carefully over the pool and joined the army of Adidas wearers marching downtown from the Upper East Side. The city claimed it was building a 2nd Avenue subway, but their coffers were empty, and the graffitied trains running down Lexington Avenue could barely contain the hordes waiting an hour on the platform. Still, I loved my new light-filled place, a railroad flat built in the nineteenth century for immigrant families serving the large households by the East River. At the west end a door opened to the living room overlooking 2nd Avenue. Through the other door, at the east end by the airshaft, was the great square kitchen with its tin-stamped ceiling, where children would have gathered at a long table and listened to Papa intone the blessing. All the rooms listed toward the stairwell. Pictures hung crooked. While winter still lingered, I got handy at wrapping a wet towel around the heating pipe that ran floor to ceiling next to my bed. In the middle of the night I plucked the dry, crusty towel from the pipe, sleep-walked through the middle rooms to the kitchen sink, soaked the towel, rewrapped it, and drifted off to the susurrus of escaping steam. When summer came I opened the windows and let traffic roar through my sleep.

I paid rent in person at a Persian rug gallery on Madison at 90th, second floor. I never saw any customers shopping for rugs. A half-dozen well-coiffed young men in dark suits stood silently in the shop's corners. My landlord's name was George Arieh, but I was never certain which man he was. The super had explained to me that for tax purposes, George was officially renting the flat to his brother, Nathaniel, who then sublet it to me. Nathaniel's lease ended the same date as mine. I never saw Nathaniel. I was told he lived in Great Neck, Long Island. I didn't care. My railroad flat was like a railroad, rumbling through the night, carrying me to a place of dreams. The next summer my divorce finalized. I had a new boyfriend, Carl, who came with a whole gregarious New York family. He lived on 80th and 1st and told me I was geographically desirable. I didn't like it when he began insisting that we alternate sleeping at his place and sleeping at mine. I liked my place better. I missed Octopus, who liked to run through the railroad flat at night as if she were being chased. But we went out with

          Meditations for a New Century

Carl's brothers and their girlfriends. We called each other from work. On Sundays—the only days without car traffic—we bicycled through Central Park.

The calendar rolled into 1982 on a sheet of ice. The city's emergency switchboards were flooded with calls from tenants without heat. The rent wars were starting to kick into gear: rent control, rent stabilization, tenant protection laws. Pulling the plug on heat was one way to get rid of tenants. I never complained, no matter how cold it got, because Carl told me that if the landlord made improvements to the boiler, he'd be allowed to raise my rent. Sometimes we made our way down to the basement, where we shone flashlights around the cobwebbed furnace, trying to find the pilot. Mostly, we slept in wool socks and hats, under layers of Thermofill.

My lease was set to expire at the end of February, and I wrote to George Arieh about renewing. I pointed out the improvements I'd made: the showerhead, the rebuilt closet, the shutters to block noise from 2nd Avenue. I would pay more rent, I said. I had never been a day late with the rent. When I saw the super, I asked if he'd seen Mr. Arieh. The family, he said, was making plans for the building. I paid my March rent in person, but Mr. Arieh was not available to talk about a lease renewal. The next week, I walked home from work through melting slush. The light was just creeping back into the day. Everything seemed tinged with blue. I stepped over the urine, unlocked the heavy main door, and mounted the broad marble stairs. It had been a fine building in its day, I thought. Even for the lower classes, someone had built high walls and stamped ceilings, had accorded people a measure of beauty.

I put my key into the lock of my stairwell door. The lock did not open.

I pulled the key out. Checked it. It was the right key. I put it in again.

The door opened, but from the inside. There in my kitchen stood a man I had never seen before. Behind him was an empty cat-carrying case. Behind that was the pink Princess phone. There was nothing else in my apartment.

"Who are you?" I said. "Where's all my stuff?"

"No hablo Inglés," the man said. He handed me a bill of lading, several sheets with carbons listing everything I owned. The letterhead named a warehouse in Bedford-Stuyvesant. Then he walked out the door.

Interlude: Halloween

The parents on the Upper West Side seem particularly stressed. Sitting at my writing desk one morning, I'm alarmed by a child's cry down on the street. Two women are shepherding four kids, with their costumes, from the school across the street. The girl who's crying doesn't want to get into the SUV parked at the curb. One mother stands passive. The other is wearing a navy knit dress that refuses to zip up the back, so most of her shoulder-blade area is exposed. She keeps yelling at the girl to get into the car, the goddamn car, the fucking car. I can't make out the girl's protest—she's crying too hard—but she is standing on the street side of the car, with the door open, and I worry she'll be hit. The passive mother passes the knit-dress mother a box of dress-up clothes, which she shoves into the back of the SUV. Then she comes around to the crying girl. She pulls the girl's clothes off her in one violent gesture, so the girl is standing in her underwear on the street. She pushes the girl into the car and slams the door. The passive mother waggles her fingers, crosses the street, and gets into her own SUV, with no children.

I'm shaking. I can't work. I keep seeing that naked girl, her thin shoulders, her face blotchy with crying. The old hymn comes back to me: *There is a balm in Gilead, to heal the sin-sick soul.*

Carl's Place

That night in March 1982, Carl came over to change the locks on both my doors. We found Octopus hiding underneath the refrigerator. I called the police, who told me the bill of lading was an eviction notice. I pointed out the warehouse name, the list. They told me to come by the next morning. Carl, the cat in the case, and I went out to dinner. When we came back, the locks had been changed again. That night, Octopus and I slept at Carl's. Next morning at the station, no report of my call or complaint existed. My boss gave me the name of a tough lawyer, Mindy, who took my case. Did I have a place where I could stay, Mindy asked, until we could put the screws to this son of a bitch?

The entrance to Carl's place was down a narrow, dark hallway where he'd hung all his clothes and propped his bike. He had two rooms, not much bigger than my horse stalls, on either side of a tiny, lightless kitchen. The place smelled of sweat, mold, and the bakery across the airshaft. He had installed high shelves in the hallway—anticipating, he said, that I might have to move in.

I was lucky. That winter had seen thirty-six thousand homeless in New York City. Articles appeared describing the underworld below Grand Central Station, the children who were waking seven stories below earth and climbing upward to attend public school. Still, I felt homeless. I contracted shingles, which the doctor explained was a form of herpes brought on by stress. Not contagious, he assured me, and not the same as genital herpes. Still, I felt scabrous, untouchable. At Mindy's urging I spent money on clothes and kept the receipts. I didn't know what to buy. Winter was giving way to spring; I looked confused in stores. When the clerks asked me what I was looking for, I said, "Everything."

Sometimes I walked back to Carl's place from work humming the old spiritual, about the soul.

Act homeless, Mindy instructed me. Spend a night at a hotel.

The Hotel

At the Gramercy Hotel, next to the locked park, my hands trembled as I passed my credit card to the clerk. I made $17,000 a year. In the brief three years of my marriage, I'd watched my ex-husband throw away the $400,000 he had inherited. The Gramercy cost $175 a night. Pillows and comforters mounded the bed like cake frosting. Carl called this our honeymoon, but in bed we quarreled for the first time, about Mindy, who he thought should be moving faster. Finally, dutifully, we made love. Next morning we ate in the sunlit breakfast room downstairs. We took the key from the clerk and entered the tiny park, our main reason for choosing this hotel. The tulips were up, Easter-egg colors with fine stars of gold or black deep inside their chalice of petals. Bees buzzed. I told Carl I didn't want to stay on at his place. Getting my things back could take a long while. I wasn't doing well in the antlike space, and Octopus was going mad. He said he should sublet his place, then, and we should look together, because I wasn't safe with the landlord's goons around.

The Tub in Kit

We knew right away we'd made a mistake. We'd paid a month's finder fee plus first and last rent, and the apartment—a block from Carl's, toward the river—had no more square footage than his. But it had a large south-facing window that Octopus sat in as the days warmed.

In May, Mindy got a warrant for me to retrieve my lease from the warehouse in Bedford-Stuyvesant. I took the subway downtown to the A to Brooklyn, to the G, then walked twenty blocks in pouring rain to stand in the anteroom of a boarded-up building while a large man smelling of wet tobacco squinted at the warrant and hawked into a spittoon. Through a yellowing partition I could see boxes and racks of clothing cramming a large storeroom. One by one, the boxes into which someone else had packed my belongings made their way down. I was allowed to look through them but not to take any of what the warrant called my *chattel*. The Ariehs were claiming I'd rented the flat furnished, and so everything—the console piano my father gave me when I was six, the antique rocker I'd restored myself, the pots and pans, the books, the stupid porcelain animals I'd set up on my dresser everywhere I'd lived, the letters from my ex-husband—belonged to them. Finally I seized on the file with my sublease and Nathaniel Arieh's lease and raced back through the rain and subway to the court hearing, already in progress.

The Ariehs were not there. But their lawyers produced a lease for Nathaniel that was different from the one I had—a two-year lease, which gave him the right to claim the flat back from me. The judge banged his gavel for an adjournment. Mindy turned to me. "You should do this," she said. "You work in publishing."

"Do what?" I said.

She had me call Julius Blumberg, manufacturer of lease forms. Mr. Blumberg's assistant took down the number of the form, dated February 28, 1981, that the Ariehs had submitted to the court. I shut my eyes after I hung up. I saw my green plastic spatula, the sweater my mother had knitted. Glimpsed in their boxes, sent back into the firetrap in Bed-Stuy. Then Blumberg's assistant called back. "I remembered something about that form," she said, "and I was right. It was supposed to be released in February 1981. But there was a typo. We scrapped it and went back to press. It came out in May that year."

When I'd hung up again, I folded my arms on my desk and put my head down. Blood pumped through my neck. We had them.

That night I took the big sheet of plywood off the bathtub and ran it full of hot water. "Tub-in-kit" apartments were only for intimate couples: The claw-footed bathtub sat in the kitchen. When we wanted to chop vegetables, we used the plywood shelf. When we needed a bath, we stood the plywood against the wall. Carl was grilling fish as I soaked in the tub, telling him what would happen now, how I would get my place back, all my things. Then, as in a dream, I was standing on the warped linoleum kitchen floor, my arms over my breasts, screaming. In the tub, a rat churned circles in the cooling water. After Carl had calmed me down, I realized I'd seen the whiskers, twitching in the overflow drain, and leapt out.

Raw Space

Settling the case took a long time. Carl kept yelling about what a bad lawyer Mindy was. I felt guilty. I should have been grateful to him. Without him, where would I have gone? The *East Side Express* interviewed me. It turned out that the Ariehs had bought the block full of railroad flats and were planning to tear them down. Their money came from Iranian oil; the whole family had arrived, the year before, on the lam from the Ayatollah Khomeini. I had just happened to be the first to try to renew my lease. The Ariehs, not considering that a single woman had legal rights, had thought I would just go away.

At last, in August, the court found George Arieh guilty. The judgment gave me $30,000, the keys to the railroad flat, and a document entitling me to its full-time use, rent-free, for the rest of my natural life. Maybe, I thought, with $30K, I could buy a condo. I looked at places in Tribeca, where several dozen warehouses had emptied in the city's recession. I could talk to Jimmy at the bar on the corner, I was told. Jimmy had raw space to sell. Jim took his thick ring of keys and unlocked the metal door of an abandoned warehouse. We rode up in the freight elevator. He showed me a cavernous, high-ceilinged area, knocked back to the studs, maybe two thousand square feet. I could have it for $50,000, he said, and he would hold paper for me.

I walked around the space. The windows were enormous, gray with embedded smoke. No plumbing, no heat, no electricity. Jimmy said he could get me contractors. I saw what someone would do here: They would transform the space into an elegant loft apartment, sleeping quarters up a spiral staircase, an open kitchen with brushed-nickel furnishings. In twenty years, they would be able to sell it for at least $2 million. I was twenty-eight years old. The person who would have this great adventure, this great good fortune, would not be me.

Carl and I looked at a couple of places in Carroll Gardens. But that was Brooklyn, and no one lived in Brooklyn unless they had a family or had been born there. For $30,000 down, the pickings in Manhattan were getting slimmer by the day. In a handful of years, they would shrink to nothing.

The Second Place, Again

You have to move back to the apartment anyway, Mindy said. Otherwise, they'll countersue.

On a muggy, late-summer day, Carl and I reentered 2nd Avenue. The place was unchanged except for the three dead plants hanging in the west-facing windows. Movers delivered my desk, bed, piano, musty clothes, the boxes I had not packed. Taking emptied containers down the stairs, I ran into the super with the gold tooth.

"How you doin?"

"Okay," I said.

"You should be careful."

That hot night, the heat came on. The next night, the same. The third night, I came home to the kitchen door ajar. This time, Octopus was under the bed. On top of it was my small jewelry box, turned upside down. Three items were missing: the sapphire earrings my father gave me for my twenty-first birthday, my grandmother's gold bracelet, and the enamel brooch my godmother passed on to me, engraved on the back with six generations of godmothers and goddaughters. The police who came over said it looked like an inside job. They suggested a safe-deposit box. When I saw the super again, he said, "I told you to be careful."

"Don't you realize I won?" I said. "I have this apartment free for the rest of my natural life."

"Which, if you're not smart, will prove to be very short," he said.

My heart was a stone dropped into water. I climbed the stairs back to my apartment. I sat at my desk and let the late afternoon light wash over me. The floor beneath me tilted like the deck of a boat. I would have to leave this apartment, and Carl, and New York, and I would never come back.

Interlude: Leaving, 2019

The day before my sublet ends, I take a walk up 2nd Avenue. At the corner of 84th Street, a twenty-five-story building fills the block. An elderly woman asks what I am staring at. "I used to live here," I say. "But it was different."

"Everything was different," she says.

George Arieh went to Rikers Island for a while, for perjuring himself in court with a phony lease. Now, more than a third of

Manhattan's "high end" real estate is owned by foreign nationals, and more by shell companies. No one pioneers in Soho lofts. If someone pees in public, it's quickly hosed away. The herpes epidemic has passed. AIDS patients drink their cocktails. The subways run regularly. The 2nd Avenue line has finally been built, though the young people, who live in Brooklyn, won't be using it. The nostalgia I feel is nostalgia for a sin-sick soul. Still, as I take the train home to Connecticut, my feet on my suitcase, I carry a little of that time back with me. I can shut my eyes and inhabit those spaces in New York again, those years spent as if in the body of a whale, always seeking air.

 Meditations for a New Century

Meditation on a Mask

What was it like? our grandchildren will ask. Wearing the masks—how was it?

It was like being underwater, we may say.

Or we may say, It lasted such a short time. We don't really remember.

Some among us may say, We were victims of the State.

Others will call it a liberation.

Perhaps they won't ask. They won't ask because the tsunami of history has buried a couple of years of masking, a blink in time. Or they won't ask because they are again, still, wearing masks. Because the mask has become a piece of clothing, taken for granted. Because the next pandemic hit, and the one after that, and after a while it seemed foolish to keep changing the mandate.

How long ago it seems, and how absurd, that we were *sewing* masks. A way to pull together, putting the sewing machines to work. During World War II, women mended clothes rather than buying new, to save fiber for the war industry. In World War I, they sewed ambulance pillows. When the electric sewing machine made its debut in my hometown at the 1904 St. Louis World's Fair, it promised to change homemakers' lives. My 1976 Singer was handed down from my stepmother who never oiled it. When the call came to make masks, I found sturdy scraps around the house—a high-thread-count sheet ripped down the middle, the remains of a terrycloth bathrobe, the legs of a pair of jeans relegated to shorts. My friend Lois gave me a length of tightly woven red percale. The hospital had downloadable patterns. I turned my writing office into a mask factory.

I've never been a careful seamstress. I didn't press the paper patterns we used to buy from Simplicity or Vogue. I never basted. Sometime in the 1980s, clothes got cheaper. Women put their machines into a closet. The last serious sewing I'd done was in the costume shop in college, where we remade thrift-store finds. We made masks for one play. I think it was *Ubu Roi*. We took a mold of each person's face and shaped the masks out of papier-maché. When the play was over we hung the masks in the costume shop. They stared down at us, fierce empty-eyed ghosts.

The masks for the hospital were shaped like a wide-open mouth, tilting over the nose and curving along the bottom, with an opening to tuck a filter through the side. So many steps were required that I determined to work factory style—cut two dozen, sew the front seams of covers and linings, clip and press all four dozen sewn pieces, top stitch, and so on. At night I left the cut pieces out, but no elves live in my house, and come morning the pieces were still there. About a third of the way through, the sewing machine stopped. When I turned it over, a gear housing disintegrated into my hand. No one was repairing machines. Everything had closed.

Lois had taken up weaving. (Ah. Pandemic hobbies. Learning Italian. Singing karaoke to your partner in the living room. Juggling. Cooking, of course. Then there's pets, meaning that if we get through this there will be a glut of cats and dogs back in the shelters, joining all those Easter rabbits.) To hem her handwoven towels, she had bought a state-of-the-art machine, which she left for me on her porch. Now the masks flew along. Just as the automobile became a computer on wheels, the sewing machine has become a computer with a needle. Still, I cheated. When I ran out of elastic, I used the extra shoelaces that came with sneakers. My seams took unscripted zags. A few masks ended in the trash. En route to Yale New Haven hospital, I stopped at one house where the seamstress was just finishing ear loops. Her masks were gingham with matching lining, a festive print of spring flowers, a hearty plaid, all pressed, ringed by fresh elastic, and carefully nestled in separate Ziplocs labeled Men, Women, Children. Accoutrements anyone would want to wear. I almost wept.

I reached the receiving warehouse late. I couldn't think what to do if the hospital had too many masks; I couldn't imagine what a person did with a box of face masks. "Please," I said to the foreman. We stood in a vast space where men pushed dollies loaded with medical supplies. Somewhere, Van Halen was playing. He opened my box. The other woman's masks were on top. He drew in a breath. "Gorgeous," he said.

None of us was wearing masks, then. Masks were not for the likes of us.

Over Labor Day weekend 2020, I met with my teaching assistant outdoors in the dry warmth, each of us sitting at opposite ends of a bench in the shade. The things on our faces felt stupid but I was setting an example. She told me about the nanny job she'd had over the summer. The younger child got anxious, she said. She learned to smile all the way up to her eyes, so the little girl could see her smiling behind her mask. "Like this," my T.A. said, and sure enough the skin lifted from the top edge of the mask and squeezed into little lines under and to the side of her large brown eyes.

I have a list of so-called "Bewares" that I hand out to writing students. As an example of *Beware the opaque character*, I give the sentence, "Her face was a mask, unknowable." I ask various students to describe a mask. In pre-Covid days, one student might say, "It's rubbery, with a clown face—huge smile, red nose." Another might say, "It goes over the eyes and turns up at the corners. It's covered in glitter." When we returned to classes after the first Covid wave, masked and disinfected, they pointed to their faces. It hooks over the ears, they said. Muffled by the cloth, their voices were lost in the distance between us. My point—that each of us wears a different metaphorical mask—felt trivial.

But as the months wore on, our masks grew different. Some of us just wore blue paper from China on our faces. Others, especially in election season, wore political slogans. Some wore clown smiles, or photographs of their own lower faces silk-screened onto cloth. When online retailers began marketing masks, I bought a set with replaceable filters, based on artwork like Van Gogh's "Starry Night" and Picasso's "Guernica." By the first fall of the pandemic, women began coordinating their masks with their outfits—or at least (given Zoom) their tops. At the skating rink—population six during winter 2021—a long, lithe figure skater, dressed in black, with a short filmy skirt that fluttered as she executed turns, sported an N95, white and cone-shaped. She glided, arms outstretched, like a black swan, her bill silently lifted.

As we began the second year, I began to feel naked out in public without my mask. At the supermarket I would slip a finger under the lower hem and lick it so I could separate the edges of the plastic bag for veggies.

There were the days before masks. Then the days with masks, before vaccines. Then the days post-vaccine—hooray! Hoorah!—without masks. Then the post-vaccine Delta variant time, followed by Omicron time, with masks creeping back in, like sun damage you think you've bleached until you go out in the sun and it's back, splotching your face.

When Georgia held a special runoff election two months after the 2020 elections, I went to knock on doors in a rural area. I had dog treats in one pocket, campaign literature in the other, and a bag of disposable masks to offer anyone who wanted to chat with me on their porch. I wore Hokusawa's "The Wave" and pushed my smile up to my eyes. The days were raw, rain spitting on the country roads. Only a handful of people greeted me wearing masks. Some of the unmasked invited me in. They weren't going to stand on a windy porch talking to a stranger, and I wasn't going to tell people what to wear in their homes. I stepped in, sat in their comfy chairs. I refused tea. Even when one middle-aged woman, in a trailer with her teenaged daughter, suddenly said, "Oh! Do you want me to put on a mask?" I couldn't bring myself to insist. You were foolish, my friends told me later. You risked death in order to be polite. One friend asked, "What if they were more comfortable in the nude?"

What is hidden allures. In the court of Elizabeth I, a lady could bare her breasts without shocking anyone, but naked ankles and shoulders were food for scandal. Some years ago I published a novel featuring American and Pakistani characters at a cultural crossroads. The initial cover design featured an olive-skinned woman in extreme closeup, only her nose and full lips on view. People would be offended, I told my editor. When a female covers in that society, she usually hides the mouth and nose while leaving the eyes exposed, not the other way around. In part the effect is to silence the wearer. But also, following the usual logic, by eclipsing those parts of the face, we heighten desire—the kissability of the mouth, the olfactory arousal.

Lipstick sales in 2020 declined as much as forty percent. Eye makeup, skin care, and hair products rose more than two hundred percent. That would not surprise any of the women I met in Pakistan, where gobs of mascara make up—in both senses—for what's invisible. At the university where my husband teaches, guidelines went out for students planning to engage in sex: masks on, no kissing. In *Romeo & Juliet,* only the eyes are masked:

Romeo: Have not saints lips, and holy palmers too?

<table>
<tr><td>Juliet:</td><td>Ay, pilgrim, lips that they must use in prayer.</td></tr>
<tr><td>Romeo:</td><td>Oh, then, dear saint, let lips do what hands do. They pray; grant thou, lest faith turn to despair.</td></tr>
<tr><td>Juliet:</td><td>Saints do not move, though grant for prayers' sake.</td></tr>
<tr><td>Romeo:</td><td>Then move not, while my prayer's effect I take. (Kisses her.)</td></tr>
</table>

I always had a hard time believing that people at those balls were really incognito. With masks covering the nose and mouth, on the other hand, our ability to recognize a face is apparently reduced by about fifteen percent. The effect is similar to prosopagnosia, or face blindness, where someone literally cannot recognize their closest friends by way of faces. We may not get better at this, though apparently the machines can. In 2020, facial-recognition technology recognized only forty percent of faces when the lens considered only eyes and forehead. By 2022, Apple announced that its facial-recognition "password" on iPhones would now wake up to its owner's masked face.

Is anonymity a bug or a feature? In the U.S., mask resisters complained on the basis of free expression. But nothing about the mask kept me from smiling. I could even push the smile up to my eyes, like my T.A. Hadn't most women worn masks in public, most of their lives? The female mask is consistently pleasant, smiles much of the time, uses paint to render the skin rosy and the eyes alert. Drop it, and you may stand accused of resting bitch face. Now, with an actual mask covering two-thirds of my face, I could go into resting bitch anytime I wanted.

It's never just a mask; it's always a signal. Proponents of religious veiling claim that the covered woman escapes the relentless male gaze. She's judged on who she is, not how she appears. Observant women in France have argued for years against that country's proscription on facial covering. Then, during the pandemic, those same women were enjoined for safety's sake to cover those very parts they had wanted to cover for faith or modesty. During the peak of the pandemic, in a much-circulated photo of Jared Kushner and Ivanka Trump with their children, the anomaly of Jared as the unmasked husband seemed normal in the same way that a traditional Islamic family photo might seem normal. It seemed normal, too, in the same

                                    Meditations for a New Century

way that we're used to seeing graying men in casual dress accompany women in full makeup, dyed hair, and structured clothing—a Westernized female mask, if you will. Azar Nafisi, author of *Reading Lolita in Tehran*, gives talks wearing bright red lipstick, a privilege she embraces as strongly as she condemns the hijab. Who's to say whether the lipstick unmasks her or remasks her?

The burqa worn in extremely conservative Muslim societies serves as a form of purdah, the custom by which a woman enters her marital home and doesn't leave it until death. The four sides of the garment are the portable walls of the home; the netting across the eyes, its window. Burqa-clad women seem to be not only hidden but mute, deaf, deprived of reasoning. Every time I remove my mask and feel as though I can hear again, I think of the burqa. Masked at the airport, I enter the restroom and my appearance startles me. And by "appearance" I mean not merely a face, which after all is partly concealed by the mask, but also a body. We pay too much attention to our faces, generally. Students describing characters in their fiction land on hair, eyes, possibly noses. They forget how revealing a set of shoulders, how specific a way of carrying one's paunch, how tell-tale a stride can be.

William Congreve wrote that "open truth" was the best mask for lying and nakedness the best disguise. I would amend that. The naked face may, indeed, be the best mask—after all, we look at ours every day and have had a lifetime to shape its expression as we prefer. But go to a nude beach or a naturists' camp, and you find individual personalities in backsides. You also find that any appearance, masked or naked, derives its character as much from the viewer as the viewed. In the coming-of-age classic *A Separate Peace*, we learn that the narrator's frenemy at boarding school "weighed a hundred and fifty pounds, a galling ten pounds more than I did, which flowed from his legs to torso around shoulders to arms and full strong neck in an uninterrupted, unemphatic unity of strength." Envy, in Knowles's description, colors the protagonist's view of his friend's body. That so many Asian faces have for so long been described as mask-like says far more about non-Asians' attitudes toward Asians than it does about Asians' intentions to hide their so-called true selves.

In movies, men wear the masks. Darth Vader, Zorro, The Mask, Batman—the list goes on, with very few women. Rip off the mask, and

                    Meditations for a New Century

the man underneath is instantly, sometimes horribly, recognizable. Masking women in movies seems silly; under one guise we'll simply find another, and there's always the risk of smudging makeup. The exception that comes to mind is Arya, in the long-running series *Game of Thrones*, who learns from a wizard how to absorb the essence of a dead person whose face she dons. Leaving aside the technicalities of this magic, what sets Arya apart from other women is her gender queerness. She dresses as a boy, passes for a boy, fights like a man, and has no interest in feminine wiles. Someone out there has noticed: Today, there's an online store selling Arya Stark masks for the pandemic, with slogans like "A Girl Has No Smile" and "Not Today, Corona."

Another generalization: Women mask up to allure or protect; men mask up to steal or frighten. Some Black men resisted masks out of the reasonable fear that police and other racial profilers would associate their mask-wearing with threatening behavior. With other resistant men, though, I wondered if they just weren't as accustomed as women to being told what to cover up and when. Early in the mask-mandate era, health advocates stressed how masking protected others. Later, they switched to stressing how it protected the mask-wearer. But caregiving is women's work, and being frightened of a teeny virus is unmanly. Macho guys will save the mask for the day they mount their charger and lower their visor.

Too bad they haven't read the studies conducted the summer of the coronavirus outbreak, which showed that a whopping eighty-eight percent of adult women in the United States found men sexier with a mask on. Across both sexes, in fact, a broad study showed that our "attractiveness rating" increases forty-two percent with a mask on. It's not just the erotic value of what's hidden. It's also that our weak chins, our crooked smiles, our marionette lines all vanish, leaving our comparatively magnetic eyes. Unfortunate, then, for the men straying onto naughty dating sites like Ashley Madison that if they choose to disguise their photo with a mask, their only option is the Zorro approach, occluding the eyes and leaving their faithless grins and double chins on view.

In Tokyo, people like to point out, masks are a part of urban life. Somewhere lies a presumption that the Japanese are more compliant. But even post-vaccines, I saw the citizens of Paris and Naples masking up, outdoors, in vicious heat, on sidewalks where no

                    Meditations for a New Century

one was within ten meters. My husband and I were walking with American friends behind Paris's city hall when a gendarme approached my friend's husband and told him to put his mask on. The husband proceeded to argue. He was fully vaccinated; the day was hot; there was almost no chance he would infect anyone, and no one could infect him. "C'est obligatoire, monsieur," the gendarme said patiently while we dragged the husband away and made him loop the elastic bands over his ears.

"C'est obligatoire." In English we would say, "It's the law." The degree to which that statement suffices depends on the social compact. The laws we consider legitimate are the ones we agree with, even if we don't like them. The sociologist Max Weber argued that people accept legal authority to the extent that they trust the underlying system that gave rise to the laws in question. I don't know of any hard data to support the idea that the French or the Japanese trust their governing systems more than Americans trust theirs; I only know that trust in the American system has eroded conspicuously since the days of Walter Cronkite and long lines for polio vaccines. It's hard to imagine responding to an American mask refuser with "It's the law." The refusal itself is testimony to the individual's scorn for the system that produced such a law. We end up, instead, imploring compliance on the basis of fellow-feeling, of altruism—of norms, that is, which we hope still hold.

That's what makes the masks tiring. Not the limits on oxygen intake. Not the fogging-up of glasses. Not the way your throat goes dry and your breath begins to smell bad after a half-hour in a mask. But this straining after some sense of community that feels evermore evanescent. With the masks on, we don't know each other; with them off, we don't trust each other.

Hawthorne gets to our ambivalence in his unsettling story "The Minister's Black Veil." We never learn why Parson Hooper has decided to cover his face. What we do learn is that the community cannot look on him without fearing for their public image and the exposure of their private shames. Like anti-maskers crossing state lines to a bar with no mask requirements, they are "conscious of lighter spirits the moment they lost sight of the black veil." Where Poe's "Masque of the Red Death" reifies contagious disease as a costume, Parson Hooper's veil serves as a rebuke of the villagers' blithe hypocrisy. When I walked into a newly reopened theater and

          Meditations for a New Century

saw rows of people all masked up, I felt a little of that same frisson—as if the sea of masks themselves, not the virus particles that might have lurked behind them, were announcing my secret contagion.

As I write, air travel to and within the United States no longer requires face covering. Apparently a flight attendant who got the news mid-flight walked down the aisle with a trash bag, singing "Throw away your masks!" During a long three-leg flight from rural France to the Midwest, I toggled between wearing my N95 and pulling it off and felt uncomfortable both ways. The air felt tinged with virus. The air felt tinged with judgment. Ninety percent of my fellow travelers were unmasked. From the look of the crowd as we moved sluggishly through the line toward passport check, you'd think the world had simply snapped back into place. We few who were masked were the spoilers.

But on the last leg of the trip, I sat next to a woman who was traveling for the first time in two years. I kept my N95 on so she wouldn't feel more anxious than she already did, judging by the surgical mask and face shield she wore. Attendants served juice and pretzels. Lifting one or the other, the woman's hand collided with Plexiglas. I recalled the glass pane protecting the judge who presided over a burglary trial for which I was considered for jury duty, back in September 2021. Three dozen of us had entered the courthouse that day, masked to various degrees—bandanas, cloth, KN95. In the courtroom, the judge asked the defendant, also behind Plexiglas, to remove his mask and face all of us. We were to let the court know if we recognized this man or had had any dealings with him. The judge's unmasked features were strong and assured. Whatever artificial protection he had from the rest of us, he looked as though he didn't need a mask the way we did; as if, like Jim Carrey in *The Mask*, he had discovered that whatever qualities the mask bequeathed him could be summoned simply by sitting in his leather swivel chair, a couple of feet higher than his audience. The defendant, by contrast, peeled his mask off slowly, reluctantly. When he faced us, a wave of shame swept through the courtroom, as if he had been asked to strip naked while we, clothed, regarded his most intimate parts and found them wanting.

I wasn't picked for a jury that day. I spent the day on the fourth floor, where a small auditorium provided jurors with decent seats and a television showing *Judge Judy* for several hours. In times past, the one perk of jury duty was the chance to encounter people from all walks of life; now and then, a pair of prospective jurors extended their acquaintance to dinner and beyond. To be human is to seek out other humans, to know ourselves by way of the current that passes between and among us. But we sat isolated, silent, either scrolling through our phones or watching the legal shenanigans on TV. Conversation felt awkward and laborious, not just from the risk of being misheard, but also from feeling that not enough oxygen passed through our filters to cope with the tensions that would arise. I slipped away to the "Quiet Room," where one bookshelf held puzzles and another paperbacks. I picked something to read. Removing my mask, I imagined telling the ones who come after: This is what it was like. When you were alone your nose and mouth disappeared. When you were alone, you could breathe.

 Meditations for a New Century

Meditation on Fire

How long ago it seems already, the day Notre-Dame Cathedral burned, the day that seems, now, to have launched our final, relentless burning, our trial by fire.

In autumn 2018, I had a job in Paris that kept me up nights. Back at my little flat in the Cinquième, I'd be on the phone with colleagues in the States until close to 11 p.m. Afterward, I'd pour my second glass of red wine, dig something out of the narrow fridge to eat, then take a walk along the Seine to clear my head before trying to sleep. The crowds that came to swing dance along the Quai des Bernardins had gone home. The tourist boats were moored farther east. Sometimes a desultory juggler tossed flaming torches along the Quai de la Tournelle. But there hulked Our Lady of Paris, her buttresses lit by gold, her square towers dark against the dense taupe of the Paris night sky.

I had a lover, that fall, who wanted to climb to the top of the towers. Finding myself generally among older people, I had made it only as far as the massive bells, at the towers' base, so I was eager. Tickets for the climb were free but hard to come by. Fortunately, I had an app on my phone. What I didn't realize, until after we had slept in and I had fixed croissants and coffee, was that the app required you to show up for the queue ten minutes before your assigned slot. We threw on clothes, clattered downstairs, used our apps to unlock two rental bikes, and sailed by the shuttered stalls of the bouquinistes. "Bon, bon, ça va," the guard said as I breathlessly begged our way in. The climb that morning felt like a stroke of luck, the kind of poorly planned success only kids get away with. From the very top, Paris spread below us like a giant circuit board. Thanks to smartphone apps, we stood on stones placed eight hundred years ago. My lover and I grinned at each other, dizzy and foolish. Notre-Dame had made us young.

A few months after I left the city, the cathedral burned. I stayed glued to the computer streaming images, to my friends' cell-phone messages. Fire not birthed by human error still leans on it for sustenance: An inexperienced guard had misread the location of the alarm, giving the fire a healthy head start. As I watched on the screen, the crackling spire fell through the burning roof, into the nave far below. "Please," I whispered to the streaming video. "Please. Not now." Under the roof, I would understand later, laced the Forest, beams from 13,000 trees harvested in the 13th century and hoisted upward by pulley and sheer human labor, to hold together and protect the bulk of the new cathedral. The Forest, one firefighter would later explain, was like a heap of dry kindling in a massive stone kiln.

As cameras swept across the puny human efforts to contain the fire, they paused now and then on the north tower, the one I had climbed that rushed, sunny morning with my lover. A spit of orange glinted from one of the lower, east-facing archways in the tower. The glint retreated. Then it crept forth again, a bright orange finger in the window, taunting us. Pumping water from the Seine to shoot toward the roof, firefighters aimed a plume at the north tower that fell short. The lick of orange danced in the window. I pictured a gremlin, a little fire man, teasing the weak arc of water and the humans who wielded it. *Come and get me.*

Who has not known fire?

Twenty years ago, I lived with my husband and two sons in a small town in upstate New York. It was June, but a cool June. Locals said there were two seasons in that part of the state: winter and July. We had shut all the windows in our house, a Federal colonial near the center of town, built in 1875 and run for many years as a funeral home. I had a job at a nearby college, but my husband struggled with mental illness and had trouble finding work. We'd picked up the house for a song, and he and a buddy had spent six months rehabbing it— knocking walls back to the original graceful archways, constructing a kitchen, rewiring, installing an upstairs bathroom, sanding and polishing floors. When we ran out of money, I'd insisted he fire his buddy. My husband eventually took a job selling mutual funds from a small office two hundred feet from our front door. We loved the house, the town, the safe life for our kids.

                    Meditations for a New Century

That June, one of my colleagues was due to give birth the same week she had planned to teach a one-day class for Elderhostel, at a conference center fifty miles away. I'd agreed to take her place. I rose in the cool morning, fixed coffee and toast, shook my husband awake, and reminded him that he would be responsible for getting the kids off to school. Four hours later, as I stood before a dense semicircle of memoir-writing senior citizens, a receptionist ducked into the room and handed me a slip of paper. *Call home ASAP*, it read. *Not an emergency.* One of the boys must have fallen at recess, I thought. Broken an arm. I waited for the lunch break, then found a phone.

"There's been a fire," my husband said. "It's out, now. But it's pretty bad."

If they lose the north tower, I thought as I kept watching the orange flame dart out of the window—growing, now, growling back at the water—they will lose the cathedral. This thought tore me in a way I will never fully understand. Many have written of the Notre-Dame fire, of how Notre-Dame is more than a house of worship, more than a historical monument, how it contains in some way the heart of France, the heart of Europe. But I am not European, or Christian. I have spent many hours inside the cathedral, have crossed its parvis hundreds of times, but I cannot count myself among those for whom Notre-Dame has intimate meaning. Still, as I watched, I thought I would not be able to bear it if Notre-Dame fell. I kept seeing those golden lamps across the dark water, the heavy lightness of the buttresses, the guardian strength of the towers atop which I had stood only six months prior.

Stepping into the vast space of the cathedral in 1940, when Paris feared the onslaught of German artillery, Julien Green found the usual silence along the floor of the nave.

> High up in the transept, however, a mighty tumult raged. The panes in the great rose-window on the north side had been removed, and in their place was a large piece of sheeting into which the wind plunged with a kind of muffled blast resembling cannon fire. They were the last gales of the winter and they were shaking the huge grey canvas as if to break it into little pieces.

That in the rage of war, the French would have taken the time painstakingly to secure from the threat of artillery thousands of pieces of medieval glass had moved me to tears when I stood inside Notre-

Dame on a sunny day. Now, though, we had failed to prepare for the threat most likely to strike her heart: fire.

"God gave Noah the rainbow sign. No more water; fire next time." That's the line from an African American spiritual that gave James Baldwin the title of his book. Water and fire—both symbols of death and of birth. But Baldwin meant to issue a warning. We fear fire more than water for a reason: We cannot swim in it. Yes, fire may split seeds to renew the forest, but it kills hideously and without mercy. My brother-in-law chose fire for his suicide. He left the insurance paperwork on the kitchen counter for his wife, stepped onto the back patio, doused himself in gasoline, and lit a match. By instinct—which I suppose those Buddhist monks in Vietnam trained to overcome—he ran from the very blaze into which he had made himself. A neighbor saw a man on fire tearing down the sidewalk and flew out to cover him with a blanket. My brother-in-law's patron saint had died by fire. But the greater reason for his choice, it seemed from his note, was to punish himself, to enter the maw of death in the most painful way possible.

It is a relief to think that most victims of the stake died of smoke inhalation before the fire could burst their skin. But I don't know if that is true. It wasn't, for my brother-in-law. A nurse gave him morphine at the hospital, to ease his passage.

When I got back to our burned home, the fire trucks had left. A van from ServPro was parked in our driveway. Inside, the house stank of wet ash. The kitchen was obliterated. Soot blackened the walls of the living and dining rooms. In our bedroom, directly upstairs from the kitchen, a charred hole showed where the fire had been poking through. Another fifteen minutes, the firefighters told us, and we would have lost the house.

My husband had left his bagel in a toaster that had already burned countless slices. Getting the kids off to school was almost more than he could manage, and when he'd shooed them out the door he'd glanced at his watch, realized he had five minutes before the opening bell on Wall Street, and dashed out to his office down the street, leaving the bagel. The rewiring of the kitchen had not included grounding the circuits.

Directly across our street lived a neighbor who took his coffee

   Meditations for a New Century

on the porch and gossiped with whoever was walking by. As he and another neighbor exchanged pleasantries, they heard a loud crash coming from our house. "Now, that's none of our business," he said to the alarmed person, and they went on discussing the gazebo on the town green.

Next door, a young teacher rented the upstairs from the home's elderly owners. She had just taken a quick shower and was surprised to see the window steamed up. Then she realized it wasn't steam: It was smoke, seeping out the edges of our upstairs windows—the fire, starting with the short in the toaster, licking the cupboard above and sizzling inside the wall, then seeking upward for the oxygen we had denied it by closing all the windows. She threw on a dress, called the fire department, and ran to our front door. Smoke alarms screamed and someone scrabbled at the door from the inside. A child, she thought, but when she yanked the door open our dog burst out along with a cloud of smoke.

The porch-sitting neighbor, seeing this new activity, roused himself, strolled down the street to the mutual-funds brokerage, tapped on the door, and said to my husband, "Excuse me, but your house is burning down."

Houses burn. Cathedrals burn. People burn. Forests burn. Even rivers—remember the Cuyahoga?—can go ablaze. In my twenties, I was living in Santa Barbara, California, when Los Padres National Forest caught fire. I first glimpsed it coming home from a picnic to the north of town, at Cachuma Lake—a glorious, warm, deep blue evening, our faces burnished by the sun, our bodies languid. To the southeast, in the mountains, a burst of tangerine orange, then another. "Fire," we said. Five minutes later came the sirens.

From town, that night, we watched as the orange sparks grew to a line across the top of the dark peaks. Then smoke obscured the blaze. Fire is hot, but burning mountains suck the heat from the valleys below and belch forth a dense haze that blocks sunlight. For the week of the fire, we town dwellers felt cold, a strange, damp, ashy kind of cold, like the cold of a sepulcher. I began gathering money from neighbors, picking up provisions at the market, and dropping them off at the firehouse, where men were cycling in from fifteen-hour shifts. "If it jumps Alameda Padre Serra," people kept saying. There was an incantatory rhythm to it, *Alameda Padre Serra*, a long name for a long road that twisted along the edge of town through the foothills by the national forest. Already officials were evacuating Montecito, where the swells lived in their architectural marvels amid views of the bay. If the fire were to leap across Alameda Padre Serra, up by the mission, we could lose the town. I fell asleep in the sulfurous cold, thinking what a narrow road it was, Padre Serra, how thin a bulwark. In the wee hours I dressed, found a twenty-four-hour market, and brought more food to the firehouse.

Five hours after fire broke out along the roof of Notre-Dame, President Emmanuel Macron stood on a makeshift stage on the Ile de la Cité and announced that the cathedral was saved "dans sa globalité." That devil of an orange flame had been the semaphore of doom. A handful of firefighters, faced with the impossibility of extinguishing the north tower's flare from the river, had volunteered to climb up into the tower, with only a narrow chance of escape if they should fail to quench the beast. They had mounted the same stairs my lover and I had taken, dragging a hose with them, and they had won the battle.

But the war continues. The photo that flashed around the world the next day showed the marble pietà before the altar, and blocking the path to it the massive, charred remains of the Forest—as if the Virgin were mourning not just her dead son but also her dead cathedral. *Dans sa globalité* means "in her entirety," but also has the context of "in her essence." Everything about Notre-Dame remains shaky. The four hundred and sixty tons of lead in its roof and spire released dust that brought lead levels in central Paris to eight times the safety limit. The great stones are still unstable on their foundation. Replacing the roof has become a political and aesthetic controversy that pits the past against the future. Something will be reborn from the ashes. But when I think back to the day I gaped at the images invading my computer screen, I remember thinking, "Please. Not now." The world in 2019, with decency and democracy under threat, felt too poised on the edge of its own precipice to endure the loss of Notre-Dame. We needed her. It wasn't right for the fire to take her.

But that there's ever a good time for a fire.

A half-dozen winters ago, when I saw smoke puffing out under the eaves of the house behind mine, I remembered the young teacher who had saved our dog, back in upstate New York. I lived, by then, in

 Meditations for a New Century

central Connecticut. I wouldn't say that the fire which flung our kitchen cupboards to the floor and gobbled up the counters was what ended my marriage. Maybe the destruction gave birth to that end; maybe it served as a crematorium for an arrangement that, undetected, had developed rigor mortis. But when I saw this neighbor's house belching smoke, I called the fire department and started across the snow-crusted back yard as sirens wailed.

The firefighters seemed to me to take their time—as they had, apparently, back in the upstate village, strapping on all the necessary gear before crossing a dangerous threshold. On this occasion they walked around the perimeter of the house. They cut the electricity. They broke a window in the front and addressed a hose to it. I approached one guy standing by the truck.

"The man who lives there is retired," I said. "He has an old German shepherd he usually walks at noon. I think they're in there."

"No one's in the house," the guy assured me.

"In the back," I said. "I think they're in the back."

They fought, the couple in that house. At five in the morning, in loud Russian. Finally, one morning that fall, my boyfriend had gone over to suggest they were waking up the neighborhood. The wife brought us a nut cake next day, to apologize.

I retreated across the damp yards to my house. Fifteen minutes later, I saw the firefighters break down the back door. They fetched a stretcher and pulled out the man. He was very stout; his belly ballooned upward. I was certain he was not breathing. I learned later that he survived, but in a compromised state. Neither he nor his wife returned to their blackened house. A cigarette, spilling from an ashtray as the man napped, had started the blaze. The dog, a firefighter told me later, didn't make it.

California is regularly ablaze, now. Long ago, the Los Padres fire stopped short of Alameda Padre Serra, and the picture-postcard town of Santa Barbara remains *dans sa globalité*. But Paradise is gone. Before the end of 2020, fires had consumed more than five million acres of the state. For weeks, the residents of San Francisco choked on the air. Fires in Australia have become apocalyptic. It's no longer a choice between fire and flood. We've got both. When the fires rage, let's face it, they present a sublime, furious beauty. There's a reason fire was stolen from the gods, a reason that God spoke out of a burning bush. A reason we love the sight of those flaming torches along the Seine, their whirling blazes reflected in the water. What's left behind reeks, to be sure. Skeletons of forests, grisly husks of civilization. We are headed there, and we show no signs of stopping.

Yet even the Christians who imagined for us the fires of hell can't resist. Think of St. Francis of Assisi addressing Brother Fire, calling him beautiful and playful, robust and strong. When my son was eight, he lit a match at my cousin's house and set a Japanese lantern on fire. We rushed to stamp it out and read him the riot act. But we all recognized the impulse: to make fire with our own hands.

Although insurance eventually covered much of the damage to our upstate home, we had to find a place to live for several months, and everyone needed clothes. As I piled heaps of smoke-saturated clothing into baskets, the stench bathed my lungs. In the summers, my hands peeled, a rare condition known as keratolysis exfoliativa, basically an allergy to one's own sweat. Handling the clothing flayed my fingers and palms. I sat before the oversized washers at the local laundromat and picked at the dead, soot-gray skin covering the reddening layers underneath. I thought what a bad time it was for this fire to have happened—the house carved up just as we'd broken free of construction projects, my husband with his new (at last!) job, now paralyzed by guilt, the boys lying awake in their temporary home, afraid that fire would take them if they slept. Over and over I rehearsed the chain of events: the bagel, the toaster, the wall, the cupboard, the four other cupboards hanging across the room, the ceiling, the counters, the dining and living rooms, the finger of flame pushing upstairs. Still, I could not comprehend how the fire had grown fast enough to take half a house in forty minutes. I ran twelve loads of laundry through the washers, three times each. A ghost of the foul odor remained, though my husband said he couldn't smell it.

One day, as we were trying to salvage what we could from the hideous house, a pretty, wan woman approached us in the driveway. She had read of our fire in the paper. She wanted us to know she understood what we were going through. She had lost her home to fire. Her son, she admitted readily when we asked, had set the blaze.

"It was the best thing that could have happened," she said. "He was schizophrenic. I couldn't afford care for him, and he wouldn't accept the diagnosis. One night while I was sleeping, he decided to

                    Meditations for a New Century

build a temple on the floor around his bed. He found a bunch of candles in a drawer in the house, and he set them all on little plates and lit them. We lost the house but we both survived. After that, the state took him. He gets the care he needs."

Something born, I thought, from fire.

And yet.

The house was never the same.
The marriage was never the same.
My brother-in-law's family was never the same.
Notre-Dame will never be the same.
A scorched earth will never be the same.

One year after Notre-Dame, the fire raging across the globe bears no flame and produces no smoke. A virus needs no fire for its birth because it is already alive, hungry, avid for our cells. *Corona* means crown, but before 2020, we heard the word mostly as a brand of beer or as the gaseous envelope of the sun, visible only during a full eclipse. Still, this moment in time feels uncannily like the spread of fire—started through a coincidence of nature, abetted by human error, and birthing in its wake the urge to restore the status quo ante.

That our world constantly changes doesn't seem to matter, while the fire or the virus rages. That it might change for the better— that the rescue of a son will be worth the loss of a house, that a wiser community will arise from the ashes of our actions—occurs to few of us. Had my house not burned, my marriage might have stumbled along to this day, wreaking much worse damage. Were the virus not flaming across America as I write, we might be looking with certainty at the looming end to our democratic experiment. And yet our dream is still to go back in time, before the fire. It will be the dream a half-century hence, when more of the world has literally burned. To take those charred remains, that hideous cracking black, and render it again into wood, into fabric, into breathing bodies, into churches and cities. If we went back, would we set the fire again? All the ingredients are there: the centuries-dry wood, the faulty wiring, the cigarette, the inattention, the story of a saint's martyrdom. Our itch to strike the match.

Meditation on the Apocalypse

I want, as always, to start small. With a grain of sand. Eternity in an hour.

Small is sentimental. It's a small, small world. A small songbird. A small monarch butterfly. A small polar bear. A small Bengali refugee. Images made for us to weep over.

Nietzsche said that natural death is "the suicide of nature, that is to say the annihilation of the rational being by the irrational." Nietzsche went mad. In Lars von Trier's remarkable movie "Melancholia," when an asteroid rushes to destroy the world, the only one facing annihilation with equanimity is a woman keenly afflicted with bipolar disorder. Death, even individual death, is too big. We shield our eyes from its glaring light. Now and then, on a crowded subway, I imagine—wait, *imagine* isn't the right word—I perceive that each individual seated or straphanging, absorbed in their phones or their newspapers or their thoughts, is condemned to death. I don't shout this out. Only the occasional mad beggar, or mad Christian, does, and when that happens we all turn our backs.

So much more difficult, then, to contemplate the slow death of the world by our own hand. The loss of one is a tragedy. The loss of billions is a statistic. It is also—in the contemporary, non-biblical sense—an apocalypse. To get people interested in forestalling this event, we rouse their sympathy by showing the photo of one calving iceberg, one drowned village, one seagull drenched in oil. We ask them to extrapolate. But I am not trying to persuade anyone. I am trying to look into the glariest light and open my eyes.

The immense privilege of the life I lead is hard to overstate. Sufficient privilege that I can debate with friends the ecological effects of air travel. Air travel! At a conference I attended on the effects of climate change, Bill McKibben pointed out that the drastic changes in the planet's air, oceans, and land mass have all been undertaken to serve one species. Let's amend that. The plastic in the oceans, the devastating warmth and its consequences, the wholesale rape of the rainforest—these things serve not one species, but one hundredth, perhaps one thousandth, of that species. I live among that tiny fraction. The very writing of this essay is a luxury. But for all the reminders to check our privilege, we who have just one life to live (and that would be everybody) seldom leap to trade that privilege for a life among the billions who will suffer most in the apocalypse.

Some years ago, I ghost-wrote a wealthy man's memoir. Bill was a billionaire out of central casting—the mansions, the yacht, the private plane, the servants, the big belly. His indulgences seemed extreme. For instance, to help research and record his life, he had a staff of fifteen museum-level archivists working on the top floor of his private suite of offices, one of whom was assigned full time to me. Bill kept four pilots on retainer for his airplane so he could get anywhere in the world on a moment's notice. I was tempted to ask one of his many subordinates how they felt, working for a man who flung money around, often for petty purposes. But no one gossiped. No one even cracked a knowing smile. My rough count of Bill's personal employees—not the ones associated with his business but just the personal assistants, housekeeping staff, groundskeepers, cook, yacht crew, and so on who helped him manage his life—came to one hundred and fifty. Mostly to procure their loyalty, each was paid significantly more for their services than the going rate. They also had spouses, siblings, children; and when one of those dependents contracted cancer or a cocaine habit, with a snap of his fingers Bill whisked them into the Mayo Clinic or rehab. In other words, by the most conservative estimate, at least five hundred people had Bill to thank for making their lives immeasurably better. Meanwhile, when Bill's business practices cost ten thousand people their jobs, including one who died by suicide because without medical insurance he couldn't cover his wife's lifesaving treatment, Bill didn't see them. Not because he was evil but because when he looked around what he saw were the five hundred grateful ones. And so Bill slept very well at night.

I cannot claim that I've improved the lives of five hundred people. Few can. But the same self-satisfaction accompanies our recycling, our attendance at rallies, our hybrid cars, our composting, and our shocked, sad essays. We look around us and see that we have done good. We cannot see farther. We cannot hear the voices of those we make suffer.

Ursula Le Guin's famous story "The Ones Who Walk Away from Omelas" imagines a city full of "not simple" people whose rich, happy lives depend utterly, and consciously, on the misery of one child who must remain shackled and miserable in a cold basement pungent with his own feces and vomit. Almost all of them accept this condition and move on. Those who do not accept it "walk away": "The place they go towards is a place even less imaginable to most of us than the city of happiness. I cannot describe it at all. It is possible that it does not exist. But they seem to know where they are going, the ones who walk away from Omelas."

The convenience of Le Guin's story, and of the William James hypothesis that inspired it, is both the singularity of the child and the ritual each citizen goes through in encountering the child. The happy citizens can say that they know the price of their happiness while both its inevitability and its low frequency—one miserable child, thousands of happy lives—give them cover. In the actual lives of the privileged, circa 2020, neither of those conditions obtains. The child is not singular—it is thousands of species, millions of refugees, entire cultures. Nor do we encounter them and their suffering, partly because the world is so vast and partly because we have a deep linguistic tradition of renaming and disguising suffering and its causes. Species "go extinct," like lightbulbs switching off, not like whales racked by starvation. We keep our data in "the cloud," not in huge energy-sucking facilities. Even "recycling," with its handy triangular logo, misnames and reduces the problem, so that in dropping our plastic bottles into a blue bin we forget that every plastic bottle must be made from new polyvinyl chloride, which comes from fossil fuel. We make playgrounds and fleece sweaters from plastic bottles, but we don't make plastic bottles from plastic bottles. As to where those fleeces and plastic playgrounds eventually go—well, that's not as accessible to our consciences as the kid in the basement.

Greta Thunberg would surely be among those who walk away from

Omelas. She began her school strikes for the climate in Stockholm when she was fifteen and sparked a worldwide movement of passionate young people. Naturally, like Malala Yousafzai, she became a celebrity. We admire her, just as we admire the stoic souls in the story who refuse a compromised Paradise. This admiration pisses her off royally. In our no-planet-B situation, walking away from Omelas is not an option. Thunberg doesn't want adults' praise; she wants their action. If they refuse to act, she warns, "We"—meaning her entire generation—"will never forgive you."

That Thunberg has a diagnosis of Asperger's may be, as she claims, her superpower. But I've noticed two things since her celebrity burst forth. One is that more images show her smiling, projecting hope. The other is that, in unguarded moments, she looks to be on the edge of a nervous breakdown.

I suspect the buoyancy constitutes a wise adjustment to the battle plan. People respond to hope. When Thunberg says, "To make great change we need everybody," she sounds much more inviting than when she says, "None of you is actually doing anything." But if the latter constitutes her true belief—that she is doomed to play Cassandra to a world of Troy—the very need to project hope surely grinds her down. In recent images she looks older and more tired than her years would indicate. When she tried to participate in a rally ahead of the World Economic Summit on Climate Change, the press of people trying to get access to her, as if she were the Virgin Mary, become so alarming that she had to be spirited away within a cordon of supporters who linked arms. Gandhi, I believe, had the same problem. But Gandhi was facing only the Goliath of colonial dominance. Thunberg is facing the revenge of Nature itself. She is capable of confronting the enormity of our malfeasance. I am capable only of concern for her personally.

Once again, in trying to speak of the apocalypse, I have reduced it—to a teenaged girl, to a Katniss Everdeen heroine, to a story. And such stories do not usually end well. Sophie Scholl went to the guillotine at twenty-one, the Holocaust continued, and few today know her name.

Supermarkets smack, to me, of the coming disaster. For that reason they depress me, and for that reason I think I should frequent them more. I should sit in one of those plastic deck chairs always stacked at the front, and watch the commerce. To be clear: The supermarket is a brilliant invention. The goodwife of Pilgrim fame would perish of joy to find her slaughtering, butchering, plucking, picking, reaping, peeling, pressing, canning, fermenting, drying, milling, milking, clabbering, baking, stewing, debugging, stuffing, brining, and preserving all taken care of for her. That the percentage of food that will poison its consumer has dropped below minuscule would put her anxious mind at rest. Not to mention that it's all in one place—the packaged and unpackaged food, the baked goods, the medicines and salves, even the basic household and hardware needs. That society has evolved to produce the supermarket can be no surprise at all, for it is the supermarket that the goodwife, without even realizing it, always dreamed of.

So let us pause to acknowledge the goodness, the brilliance, of the supermarket.

In the supermarket, people condemned to death wander up and down aisles loaded to the brim with goods whose production and packaging take morsels of nature and violate everything that makes nature sustainable. They hunt for bargains, though food itself seems a bargain, cheaper than ever before and requiring nothing more arduous than ripping off the plastic cover to place the tray in the microwave. They fill their carts with boxes and bags as if food itself presents as boxes and bags. They do this over and over, every week, or twice a week if they can get in on Super Senior Wednesdays. Increasingly, these shoppers make their way around professional shoppers, armed with gigantic carts on which bags are neatly stacked. These people are shopping for the people who cannot or choose not to come to the supermarket. They check their phone for the items on the list, fill the bags, charge the customer, and load the orders into the van to drive around town delivering food as if food presents itself in bags on your doorstep.

Americans throw away 150,000 tons of food every day, almost as much as we consume. If global food waste were a country, researchers tell us, its impact on global warming would be second to China's. As a statistic, that's still too small. It's part of the apocalypse the way the trunk or the ear of the elephant is the elephant to one of the blind men in the old parable. The elephants, too—that is, the elephants living in the agony we have created for them—are part of the apocalypse. And we are the blind.

As a child, I sometimes dreamed of a very large object approaching me from very far away but moving so fast that I could not get out of its path. My mother told me these were ether dreams, imprinted on me by the ether mask placed on my face when I underwent adenoid surgery at four. I recall them when I try to apprehend the apocalypse. Time, distance, velocity: If we could get these in alignment, even fleetingly, we might catch a whiff of what's befalling us. We who have the luxury to bemoan air travel have adjusted our sense of distance. We grasp how Greenland matters to Florida, how small the ocean really is compared to the size of the burden we've tossed its way. But in recalibrating distance, we may have lost our sense of time and velocity. That is, we think we can move fast, and a decade hence is an eternity. As the environmental philosopher Lynton Caldwell puts it, one reason we have ignored, denied, or rejected clear warnings of the consequences of our actions "may be an underdeveloped mental capacity to envision our situation on the time-space trajectory of the real world."

What if we could increase our mental capacity, could ramp up exponentially by putting our minds together? The apocalypse is upon us in no small measure because our stakes in our own families, our own little communities, little governments, little nations far outweigh our stake in the planet, and so we set ourselves in mutual opposition not just sometimes but almost as a condition of being. Consider, instead, a murmuration of starlings, a school of fish, a swarm of bees. This isn't really group consciousness, according to scientists. Each fish, bee, bird is a decentralized, self-organized system. Their collectivity gives birth to something else, intelligent global behavior that's unknown to the individual agents.

The closest approximation we have, in humans, is called herd behavior, but it's hard to argue for its intelligence. Think of large, packed crowds of protesters, or subway riders, those moments when you feel reduced to your lizard brain and your intentions are indistinguishable from the intentions of the group. Capitalism has harnessed herd mentality to manipulate things like impulse buying. Go up the scale and you get Kristallnacht, the Tulsa riots, the insurrection of January 6, 2021.

Proposition, then: Herd mentality takes over when we are not thinking straight. True or false? False, surely, if we need to stop wasting neurons quibbling about gross domestic product as our world

                    Meditations for a New Century

burns. The problem is not with the swarm itself but with the lack of will to put its power toward the rescue of the planet. No countries to conquer, in this enterprise, no fortunes to make, no undesirables to expunge.

The dinosaurs lasted one hundred and sixty-five million years. A comet, like Melancholia, ended them. Nothing they could have done. Homo sapiens has been around for two hundred thousand years, just over one tenth of one percent of the dinosaurs' reign. If you count our evolving from homo erectus, we go back two million years. If you count us as part of the primate family, we go back maybe fifty-five million years. I can wrap my head around this much: What we are doing as a species guarantees that the Anthropocene will end long before we come close to matching dinosaur tenure. So don't tell me that our big, independent brains are helpful to our survival.

I write, here, in prose. The book of "Job," a tale not of the end of the world but of the end of one man's domain, tells us something about prose. Famously, the book splits. The prose narrative recounts Job's trials, his acceptance of undeserved punishments, and his eventual reward with property and family even richer than he possessed at the start. Breaking up the narrative, though, Job's epic wrestling with his interlocutors leaves little resolved beyond Job's passionate cry, "What is my strength, that I should hope? and what is mine end, that I should prolong my life?" God, of course, eventually speaks out of the whirlwind by asking Job where he was when God made the world—a rhetorical question if there ever was one. The arguments and questions thickening the central section of "Job" require poetry, it seems, because they engage questions that nag at us, find no answers, and will not leave us in peace.

If I had the gift, maybe I could face the apocalypse in poetry. The philosopher Jonathan Lear, whose *Radical Hope* considers the destruction of Native American Plains culture, proposes poetry as a way to regain intelligibility after the collapse, the poet being "a creative maker of meaningful space." Meaningful space, in the "Job" narrative, is the space where the dialectic rages. Prose keeps insisting on a conclusion. To conclude is to turn away.

You could say we've always confronted the apocalypse. Its original meaning, in Greek, was "to uncover." To those who study the capital-

A Apocalypse of the book of "Revelation," I may be misusing a term that should involve the Second Coming and Final Judgment. "Climate catastrophe" is a popular alternative—Greek again, meaning a sudden turn or overturning. But if we measure time as human lifespan, the turn is hardly sudden, nor is anything being overturned. Processes are unfolding, according to the laws of physics, precisely as they should.

Three truths about beliefs in the apocalypse as I'm framing it:

1. They range across all cultures and throughout recorded history.
2. They generally involve previous ends of the world, particularly due to a flood.
3. Another chapter inevitably follows the apocalypse, and for some it's a better arrangement.

The second truth grabs my attention only because there's good reason to think the coming uncovering, if it doesn't arrive by fire, will arrive by flood, when Greenland and the polar caps melt into the sea. But the third truth suggests to me that my failure to face this thing square on is no worse than anyone else's. Whether we've dreaded the wrath of God or the logical outcome of natural laws, we have never really stared down our nightmare. Yes, we've got the ghastly visions of Hieronymus Bosch—the heads walking on feet, the bird-man swallowing the naked woman whose anus expels crows—but on the other side of the suffering lies redemption, for the pure or the lucky. Where the apocalypse rests inside a cyclical view of history, it gives birth to the next age of humankind; where it provides a linear endpoint, there's another world, or Paradise, awaiting those who make it through the fire. And it is with those exemplary types that we identify, naturally.

Our contemporary versions of apocalyptic narrative come in the form of books and films that provide catharsis. After experiencing the terror and the cold sweat, we emerge relieved to be whole. Mostly the heroine triumphs; occasionally, she doesn't. In "Melancholia," that comet hits. In Cormac McCarthy's *The Road*, the boy will find others, but the others are a dwindling, doomed lot. In the screen adaptation of Neville Shute's *On the Beach*, we close with a montage of empty cities. Here, the imagination is exercised toward didactic purpose. You don't want to end up like these people? Then change, damn it. As "On the Beach" silently announces, "There is still time, brother." If you won't change, at least you can live in your moment and be glad it's not the moment of the movie.

In none of these visions is the extinction of species other than human taken seriously. Yes, I know: Noah. But those paired animals, like Noah's family, survive nicely. We grow sad at the loss of beauty (the snow leopard) and intelligence (the whale) in the world, but we do not dread it on anything like the same level as our own self-inflicted fate. Maybe that's what it means to be a species—that we cast our lot, in the end, among our own. Nor does the apocalypse that I am trying to comprehend mean the actual extinction of human beings. That's far too simple, really, and the stuff either of science fiction or of that dinosaur-derived historical arc in which every species, at some point, becomes what we call extinct.

This apocalypse means, rather, that both humans and almost all other species suffer on a scale never previously known, for an undetermined time, without hope of surcease. As that suffering goes on, civilizations and societies, including the societies of other species, collapse. We will have done this to ourselves and to the planet, and we will not stop doing it until and unless we are forced to. At which time, the shriveled, drowned world will continue, indefinitely, to suffer. No end to the movie, no walking out of the theatre.

I can step back and write these words. What I cannot do is reenter the world—this world—in which we are setting in motion the chain reaction, whose outcome is the apocalypse, and look at it. Not at the same time.

The world has ended before—and by this I don't mean the comet that killed the dinosaurs or the legends of the Flood. I mean the Black Plague; I mean the genocide of Native America. To those who lived among those cataclysms, the world ended, because the world did not extend past the boundaries containing the disaster. As Plenty Coups of the Crow Nation said of the time "the buffalo went away": "After this, nothing happened." Of Florence in the Plague, Boccaccio wrote, "So grievous was the harshness of heaven, and perhaps in some degree of man, that . . . upwards of a hundred thousand human beings lost their lives within the walls."

We know only the world in which we live. Things happen in our world; destroy that world, and nothing happens. That other worlds exist, or will exist, can hardly matter. In this sense, cognizant though we may be that this time, really and truly, the entire planet is threatened, I doubt we differ in a serious way from those who understood a certain expanse of geography to constitute the world. What does it matter, for instance, for some scientist to tell me that the laws of probability suggest that sentient beings occupy some other planet heated by some other star, and that they are not destroying themselves?

I had a friend who became mentally ill. We had sung together in a chorale in Roanoke, Virginia. Along with my then-husband, I socialized with him and his wife, often going out after concerts. After I left Roanoke and my marriage, I heard that his wife had committed him to a psychiatric institution and forbidden contact with their children. He had seemed a pleasant, intelligent guy, a fine tenor, a chemist who worked in a local pharmaceutical research group. A couple of years later, on my way elsewhere, I traveled through Roanoke. He had been released from the institution, had gotten divorced; my understanding was that he had a new girlfriend, a much younger woman from Russia. I stopped by his house, where I met the woman, a sad little creature with bottle-blond hair, brown teeth, and a look of desperation. My friend explained to me that he had found her through an online agency. That she would live with him for three months before they had sex; that after they had had sex, she would live with him another three months; and if she agreed at that time, they would be married. They needed to be married, he explained, because when the Martians came to destroy most of Earth, they would take with them only those who were believers and were married, so they could relocate to Mars and repopulate the human race. When I pointed out that NASA probes had shown no life on Mars, he regarded me with condescension. The Martians didn't live *on* Mars, he explained. Eons ago they had destroyed their environment, they had devastated their planet. They lived *inside* Mars.

It is almost an article of faith that people like us—individualist, greedy, hubristic—will self-destruct. Not only religion but science fiction feeds on this notion, countered by the notion that wiser beings, like the eldila of C.S. Lewis' Cosmic Trilogy, govern their spheres sustainably and compassionately. Every such story of destruction is an exhortation. Every such exhortation falls short. The one thing worse than failing to heed the lesson is to believe it, as my Roanoke friend apparently does, as fact. What happened to him and the bride he was buying, I never knew; I did not want to know.

Still, the notion that other beings have devastated other worlds, perhaps billions of other worlds over billions of millennia, has this one advantage: It reduces the apocalypse to a small thing. The merest blip in cosmic time. I don't mean that taking a God's-eye view renders the climate crisis insignificant, any more than calculating the short span of human life on earth renders Beethoven's late quartets insignificant. Rather the opposite. We can keep our focus on a small thing. We can find the beauty in it, no matter how its fate hurts our heart. We can allow the miracle of its existence to pass away within the greater miracles around it.

In the remarkable French television series "Un village français," a Jewish teacher returns from a concentration camp with terminal lung disease. After she begs a local doctor to end her painful life, the doctor injects her with a fatal dose of morphine. As she dies, she says, "I am becoming invisible. I am disappearing. And without me, the world cannot exist." In a historical sense—and even in the series, which goes on for four more seasons—what she says is egotistical poppycock. But as a way to understand what happens when I attempt to dwell on the apocalypse, it clarifies. If the most famous phrase in philosophy is Descartes' "I think, therefore I am," one of its corollaries must be "I think, therefore the world is." The world, what anyone at any point in time calls the world, exists from a point of view, which is both necessary and partial. If I consider the apocalypse as a small event bursting with lost beauty and the consequence of hubris, I can glimpse, for a moment at least, how its very apocalyptic nature derives from the perspective of a human being detecting it on the horizon. What will take place on this spinning sphere over the next century and more is an event. What creates the apocalypse is the relation between that event and a consciousness struggling and failing, failing and struggling, to swallow a stone of grief and responsibility that takes on the size, in one's throat, of the Earth itself.

    Meditations for a New Century

Acknowledgments

Thanks to the editors of the following journals where these essays first appeared:

"Meditation on a Rat," *American Scholar*, Winter 2016

"Meditation on Pain," *Prairie Schooner*, Spring 2017

"Meditation on Needlepoint" as "A Stitch in Time," *American Scholar*, Summer 2020

"Meditation on Middle G," *New England Review*, Spring 2021

"Meditation on Figure Drawing" as "Writing the Body," *The Southern Review*, Summer 2009

"Meditation on Gandara" as "Gandara in Suburbia," *Arts & Letters*, Fall 2014

"Meditation on Hair" as "Bush," *Fourth Genre*, Summer 2011

"Meditation on Fire," *Crazyhorse*, 2021

About the Author

Photo Credit: Paul John Roberts

Born in St. Louis, Lucy Ferriss has lived on both coasts, in the middle, and abroad. The overturning of Roe vs. Wade has brought renewed attention to her frighteningly prescient novel, *The Misconceiver*, a dystopian near-future story of survival in a Christo-Fascist U.S., where laws increasingly turn against women, LGBTQ, and people of color. Ferriss's eleventh book, *Foreign Climes*, won the Brighthorse Books Award in short fiction. Other recent fiction includes *A Sister to Honor* (Penguin, 2015) and *The Lost Daughter* (2012), a Book-of-the-Month pick. Her memoir *Unveiling the Prophet* was named Best Book of the Year by the *Riverfront Times*. Her novel *Nerves of the Heart* was a finalist in the Peter Taylor Prize competition. *Leaving the Neighborhood and Other Stories* was the 2000 winner of the Mid-List First Series Award. Other short fiction and essays have appeared most recently in *The American Scholar, december, Missouri Review, New England Review*, and *Crazyhorse* and have received recognition from the National Endowment for the Arts, the Faulkner Society, and the Fulbright Commission, among others. She lives with her husband, Don Moon, in the Berkshires and Connecticut, where she has two strong sons and abiding passions for music, politics, travel, tennis, and wilderness.

Books by Lucy Ferriss

Meditations for a New Century

Foreign Climes and Other Stories

A Sister to Honor

The Lost Daughter

Unveiling the Prophet

Nerves of the Heart

Leaving the Neighborhood and Other Stories

The Misconceiver

Against Gravity

The Gated River

Philip's Girl